Custom Bicycles

A passionate pursuit

images
Publishing

First reprinted in 2010

The Images Publishing Group Reference Number: 938

Published in Australia in 2009 by

The Images Publishing Group Pty Ltd

ABN 89 059 734 431

6 Bastow Place, Mulgrave, Victoria 3170, Australia

Tel: +61 3 9561 5544 Fax: +61 3 9561 4860

books@imagespublishing.com

www.imagespublishing.com

National Library of Australia Cataloguing-in-Publication entry

Author:	Elliott, Christine.
Title:	Custom bicycles : a passionate pursuit / Christine Elliott
ISBN:	9781864704235
Subjects:	Bicycles–Customizing.
	Bicycles–Design and construction.
	Bicycles–Pictorial works.
	Skilled labor.
Other Authors/Contributors:	Jablonka, David.
Dewey Number:	629.2272
Coordinating editor:	Andrew Hall

Designed by The Graphic Image Studio Pty Ltd, Mulgrave, Australia

www.tgis.com.au

Digital production by Chroma Graphics (Overseas) Pte Ltd, Singapore

Reprinted by Everbest Printing Co. Ltd., Hong Kong/China

IMAGES has included on its website a page for special notices in relation to this and our other publications. Please visit www.imagespublishing.com.

Contents

Foreword

A bicycle frame builder is no ordinary man. He is a craftsman, an engineer, an artist, and a perfectionist, who through his extraordinary talent has produced a machine that can carry man over the highest mountains, along the narrowest roads, and over huge distances. He has given man the ability to travel under his own power at speeds in excess of 100 kilometers per hour on a machine that seems as flimsy as a balsa wood toy, yet in reality is as strong as a Centurion tank.

For more than 150 years—since Scotsman Kirkpatrick Macmillan produced a bicycle with pedals from his smithy in Courthill, Dumfrieshire—we have seen this machine evolve. Even today it continues to change its shape, wandering away from the traditional diamond frame, as these unique frame builders use modern materials in their search for more speed.

One finger is all that is required to lift a modern-day bicycle built from the lightest components known to man. A far cry from the 52-kilogram quadricycle built for Prince Albert, the husband of Queen Victoria, in the 19th century.

However this beautiful coffee-table book is not about the history of the bicycle, but instead focuses on some of the specialist frame builders who from their bases around the world produce, to this day, the finest bicycles ever made. Often made in ridiculously small workshops in the backstreets of cities around the world with little more than a blowtorch and a vision, these sleek works of art—because that is what a bicycle is—roll into the full view of the public without ever receiving the fanfare they deserve.

Many of these great modern-day artisans are listed in this book with their work bared for all to see and scrutinize. From places as far apart as Seattle and Surrey or Geelong and Grants Pass, Oregon, the pages here reveal the finest bicycles of our time. Machines designed to carry you to the shops or over the highest road in the Pyrenees—the Col du Tourmalet—are awaiting your awe.

Having raced for 12 years and reported on the Tour de France for 37, to me there is nothing kinder to the eye than a bicycle. Throughout my life, it has

carried me (not always as fast as I would have liked!) far and wide and never complained. If you can make the journey, it certainly can.

Recently, a friend of mine passed an exceptional milestone by accomplishing his 1.6 millionth kilometer in a lifetime spent logging every kilometer ridden since a boy. He was even late for a dinner we had arranged for him in his honor because he was circling the venue until that special landmark was reached.

You will love browsing through this book, even if you have little or no interest in cycling. These thoroughbreds live in their own special stable, having been produced by special people; so admire and envy their work, as they can do something that very few people in the world can do: build a bicycle.

Phil Liggett
Hertford, UK

Introduction

Custom Bicycles presents a selection of the many frame builders around the world who dedicate their lives to designing and creating beautiful, handcrafted bespoke bicycles. Each chapter visually showcases their craftsmanship with illustrations of their bikes and unique features, while the accompanying text tells of the personal journeys that inspired each designer to become a custom bicycle frame builder. The chapters offer personal insights into how their skills were developed and also feature their philosophies behind the techniques used and choice of building materials.

The featured builders range from highly experienced master builders, who have many years and hours of frame building underpinning their expertise, through to those who represent the next generation of visionary frame builders. All of the frame builders in this book have been motivated by the ambition to create bikes in their own special way, while taking inspiration from traditional designs and more experienced builders.

In a consumer-driven world where many things have a use-by date, owning a handcrafted bicycle that has been custom fitted to suit your body and riding requirements is an investment in quality and longevity and has the potential to become a family heirloom. These bikes are not only practical, human-powered machines, but works of art that make you want to throw away your car keys and go riding down a road or along a trail in search of the sense of freedom that is reminiscent of flying through the air.

Whether these bikes are referred to as bespoke, custom-made, or hand-built, the rider is always at the centre of the design, and every frame builder has their own technique for measuring a customer. The time taken to build a bike depends very much on the size of the business and design complexities. Many of the builders are lone craftsmen or work in a team of two and are able to execute every stage

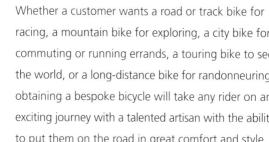

of the process through to the finished product. There are also the builders who gather a small to medium team of people together, each with a particular area of expertise. Then there are the larger companies that are able to maintain the personal, hand-built nature of a bespoke bicycle.

When it comes to preference of materials such as steel, titanium, aluminum, carbon fiber, or more exotic materials such as bamboo, they are chosen for their particular characteristics, design abilities, and intrinsic riding qualities. A bespoke bicycle can be made in any style depending on the performance needs of the customer. Some builders specialize, but most build a range of bicycles and collaborate with the customer to develop their dream bike.

Whether a customer wants a road or track bike for racing, a mountain bike for exploring, a city bike for commuting or running errands, a touring bike to see the world, or a long-distance bike for randonneuring, obtaining a bespoke bicycle will take any rider on an exciting journey with a talented artisan with the ability to put them on the road in great comfort and style.

Christine Elliott and David Jablonka

Anderson Custom Bicycles

St. Paul, Minnesota USA

Dave Anderson loves dropouts. Not for counterculture reasons, but from the point of view of a bicycle builder. His favorite feature on a bike happens to be dropouts, particularly when they are stainless, compact, smooth, and elegant. Making custom bikes seemed to be a natural path for Dave to follow, as he had always enjoyed making things from a very young age and he really loved bikes. Dave builds his custom bikes from both steel and carbon, however the majority of his bikes are made from steel because he finds that it is ideally suited to making custom frames and feels that it's the only material that really allows the builder to put his "mark" on his work: "I use the materials that I feel are best for a given situation. To a certain extent form follows function, and both form and function are heavily influenced by how I want the bike to look and perform."

Dave describes himself as a "jack-of-all-trades" and when it comes to building bikes, he is a one-man shop involved in every step of the building and finishing process. Depending on the complexity of a bike design, it can take anywhere from one to two or more weeks to complete a bike. If he is building a fairly basic design, it could take him a week including the painting. When it comes to a more complex design, where there is considerable carving, detail, polished stainless, and lots of graphics, it can take an experienced frame builder like Dave Anderson two or more weeks to complete a customer's dream custom bicycle.

Believing that everyone can benefit from owning a custom-made bike, his philosophy is reflected in these words, "A truly handmade custom bike is designed and built for you and you alone. It will fit you perfectly and will be built with materials and components that reflect you and your riding style. A good custom bike will also say a lot about you, your personal tastes, and your sense of style." With every customer, Dave is literally building a bike from the ground up to fit their body, riding style, and the purpose for which it will be used.

"A truly handmade custom bike is designed and built for you and you alone. It will fit you perfectly and will be built with materials and components that reflect you and your riding style. A good custom bike will also say a lot about you, your personal tastes and your sense of style."

"I use the materials that I feel are best for a given situation. To a certain extent form follows function, and both form and function are heavily influenced by how I want the bike to look and perform."

Full stainless frame with polished lugs and stays

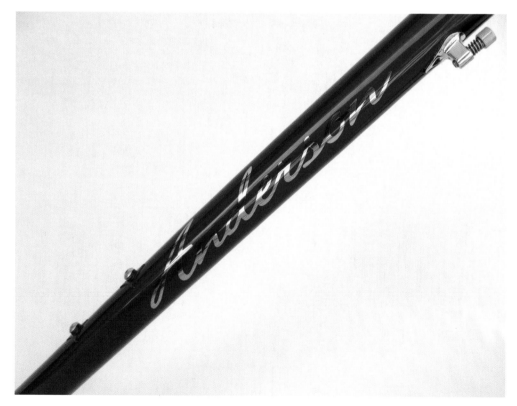

It looks fast standing still …

"I've wanted this bike for the last ten years and it was well worth the wait. I worked closely with Dave on every aspect of it. The end result is a bike that not only looks fast standing still, but one that also fits my body, personality, and riding style perfectly. Beauty is only skin deep, but this bike must be ridden hard to appreciate why I love it so much. Balance is the best way to describe it. When I grit my teeth and start swinging from side to side, it responds like no other bike I've ever ridden—and I've ridden a lot of bikes. The bike rides so well that I do not hesitate to take it on 5-hour-plus rides."

Guy Stone

Lugged Reynolds 953 stainless frame set

Atum22

Surrey, United Kingdom

Atum22 takes its name from the Egyptian God of creation, Atum, and the atomic number of titanium, which is 22. It is a commission-only bicycle company that specializes in conducting a thorough fitting system to enhance the level of cycling enjoyment for its customers. The company was born from the ideas of a sports chiropractor, who conducted measurements and consulted on ergonomics, a professional triathlete, who organized and managed each build, and a sports designer with extensive frame design experience.

Dr. Glenn Duffy's desire to understand the entire building process led him to add bike designing and building to his extensive understanding of the body's physiology. Glenn places great emphasis on conducting extensive interviews with clients as well as a two-hour fitting appointment. The discussion includes injury history, riding aspirations, and an extensive set of measurements that take into consideration flexibility, physiology, functional mechanics, and anatomy. The fitting process, delivered by someone with professional experience in biomechanics, is a distinguishing feature of having a bespoke bicycle made by Atum22: "It was once said by a customer

that Atum22 is the Savile Row of the bicycle world." The team is continually amazed at how this measure-and-fit process builds bikes that most often banish common discomforts for their customers.

During the design process, Glenn doesn't want to be limited by preconceptions or tradition and will employ whatever technique or feature best suits the customer. The design options offered by Atum22 are almost overwhelming. From internal and external cabling options, fillets, gussets, and varied tube shaping, Glenn aims to combine different elements to best harness the strengths and weaknesses of each rider. Sprinters may get extra tubing and filleting at the bottom bracket, while for Audax riders it will be longer and more flexible, creating a more comfortable rear end. Glenn also takes great care in adjusting steering geometries to each individual's riding style.

Titanium is Atum22's metal of choice because it is lightweight, offers outstanding performance and longevity, and is also corrosion resistant with amazing strength. A very elegant metal, titanium has a beautiful luster that can be finished in matt or polish. Another unique feature of Atum22 bikes is the laborious

frame-finishing processes that produce frames that are stunning without being garish. Customers can request anything from Celtic motifs to dragons to British flags, or subtle engravings of their initials or name, plus themed, colored componentry. Whatever their desire, the attention to detail is second to none: "It is often commented that we build bikes then make them look like jewelry." Glenn particularly enjoys the templates coming off after the dirty, grimy sandblast process, and polishing off the manufacturing marks. This is when the frame springs into life and the image of the final product starts to take shape. Many customers come to Atum22 to help solve a history of recurring injuries or to avoid developing a future injury, however most customers come simply to commission a bicycle that delivers the ultimate riding experience while looking stylish at the same time.

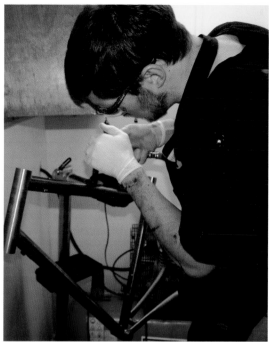

High-polish frames take up to three days of work—each customer has his or her initials engraved on the headtube

Each frame is laboriously worked to achieve a high-polish finish

Disc-specific dynamo hubs driving a cutting-edge LED headlight

"It was once said by a customer that Atum22 is the Savile Row of the bicycle world."

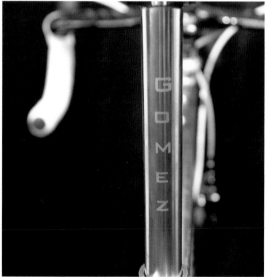

Customers can have their name etched into their seatposts

Internally routed bikes get braided cables

Everything about it is spot-on ...

"In a word it's incredible. Sunday was the first time I'd ridden it properly and it is hard to describe how good it feels. Mostly I've found with bikes one aspect sticks out—whether it be its lightness, stiffness, etc. With this bike though, there isn't one particular aspect that seems to dominate. Everything about it is spot-on. Its weight, handling, comfort, agility, and stability—absolutely brilliant. The fact that I got off the bike on Sunday after not riding for a good few months with no discomfort at all also says a lot."

Christian Holmes

Jewelry ready for collection

An elite triathlon bike awaits collection

Baum Cycles

Geelong, Victoria Australia

Darren Baum's family tell a story of him as a baby lying in a bassinette in his father's workshop and instinctively knowing to turn away as his father struck an arc. When Darren became old enough, the mechanic who worked for his father became his mentor and taught him welding, machining, and fabricating. Darren spent every night, weekend, and holiday period plus any spare moment working for him, until he eventually started working in a bike shop. At age 14, Darren Baum's first foray into bike building was a tandem built out of tubing from his father's workshop, constructed so that he and his mate could ride together in the Great Victorian Bike Ride.

It was in 1989, while Darren was still at school, that he had his first real taste of life as a frame builder. He organized two weeks of work experience with master frame builder Brian Cross and was sponsored with a Reynolds tube set. Darren was eager and keen to build his first real bike, but Brian had other ideas and was not going to let him anywhere near his tube set until he had first learnt a few essential basics. On his first day, Darren was kicked out of the workshop and told to walk around the block to have a good

hard think about why he didn't have any grease on his seat post. On his return, he had to learn how to file and was given a painted tube with several layers of different colored paint. Using a particular filing technique, Darren had to learn to file off each layer without touching the next colour. By early afternoon he had proven he could do it and said to his boss, "Can I build my bike now?" To which Brian replied, "No, now you need to learn to do it left-handed."

The hand and construction skills that Darren gained in his early years gave him an incredible jump-start into his aircraft maintenance engineering apprenticeship. During this period, Darren further extended his skills by learning how to do computations from the engineers and completed further welding training at night school. Darren is now regarded as one of the best welders in the business: "When I sit down to weld, I know exactly what the hand movements are going to be for the next 30 seconds, where I'm moving to, and where I'm going to stop." Darren finds the best time to do welding is early in the morning before the rest of the Baum team arrive, because it's very relaxing and he also likes to hear what he's doing.

Darren's whole aim, right from the beginning, was to gather the skills to become a bicycle frame builder and in 1996 the first Baum frame was sold on a commercial basis. Darren likes to make the sort of bikes that he enjoys riding, which is why he uses titanium and steel to construct his bikes. The Baum Cycles approach to the art of bike building is to create an integrated holistic design. In line with this philosophy, and in order to maintain complete control over the processes, all Baum Cycles facilities are housed under one roof in the coastal town of Geelong. When designing a bike for a customer, the most important thing to consider is what the true end use is going to be, and this may range from racing, touring, riding on a bike path, or weekend racing to the café.

All Baum bike frames are named after different types of coffees, in recognition of the changing dynamics of the riding set, which these days is more likely to be riding to a café than actually training to race. "Espresso coffee, you're there, you drink it, you get on your bike. The Espresso frame is the same, it delivers exactly what you want."

"When I sit down to weld, I know exactly what the hand movements are going to be for the next 30 seconds, where I'm moving to, and where I'm going to stop."

Darren Baum welding a titanium frame

Darren Baum stamping the serial number on a titanium dropout

Why I love my Baum …

"Rosie is named after both her color and the link to roses, and was given to me as an engagement present! To commemorate the engagement, she has a beautifully hand-painted diamond on the down tube. In addition to the obvious sentimental attachment I have to Rosie, she is an awesome bike. She rides beautifully, is smooth on long rides yet stiff when you need some speed, and seems to ride up hills all by herself. She is an amazingly versatile bike, which I've hammered up and down Beach Road, taken to the hills of the Lake District in the UK, and used for time trialing in sprint and long distance triathlons. Mostly I love her because she's unique and because she's so pretty."

Hanna Steyne

I love the brushed titanium …

"I love the brushed titanium finish and my friends are in awe of the cool workmanship on joints and cutouts. As for the ride, well it's exceptionally comfortable and easy on my commute to work—it takes all those bumps and ramps on the cycle track with ease. We've spun along Beach Road, and in the top gears it's fast and smooth. I can't wait to load the panniers and head out on a multi-day trip, where I expect it to come into its own …"

Derarca O'Mahony

Steel Ristretto track bike

Darren Baum, founder of Baum Cycles sitting in front of a titanium-framed Cubano

Romano tourer, with a brushed titanium finish

Steel-framed Espresso

"Espresso coffee, you're there, you drink it, you get on your bike. The Espresso frame is the same, it delivers exactly what you want."

Bilenky Cycle Works

Philadelphia, Pennsylvania USA

Steve Bilenky has many strings to his bow: he's been building bikes for 25 years, is a bass guitarist in a successful instrumental rock band, has a degree in agricultural engineering, and a background in industrial arts such as welding, machining, and woodwork. At first he thought he would follow a career in engineering, then went into agriculture because he likes farming, but he soon found himself working in bike shops again after finishing college. At the age of 13, he began working in shops as a bike mechanic, then eventually moved into managing the shops. By 1978, he had decided to open his own bike shop, but after running the shop for a few years he knew he wanted something more, and that something was to start making his own bikes. "Building your own frames is a bike shop owner's PhD," says Bilenky. In 1983, Sterling Cycles was launched as the brand for Steve's handmade bicycles, which was then changed to Bilenky Cycle Works in 1992.

The type of bicycles Steve Bilenky makes now are not like the more utilitarian bikes that he first rode, which were a refinement of the English three-speed roadster bike. In 1983, Steve built his first bike, a lugged Reynolds frame with five-speed Sturmey-Archer gears and high-quality components. This bike was aimed at a more refined cycling crowd, as Steve had a vision of building bikes of high-quality that were user friendly and had a certain amount of panache, "I want it to work good, but I also want it to look good." Around that time mountain bikes were being marketed as ideal bikes for everyday riding, so Steve produced a city bike called a Metro 5, the sort of bikes that are now becoming popular as commuter bikes. He is now often sought out for his advice on how to extend on the theme of building style into bikes.

The Bilenky workshop is approximately a 3-mile bike ride from his home, so Steve cycles to work each day where the team of five, including his daughter who takes care of customer service, creates a range of stylish Bilenky bicycles. Consultation with customers takes place in the workshop or via a form if they live out of town. Steve utilizes formulations that have been built up after many years of experience, works with other builders, and uses the fit-kit system. All available information then forms the basis for sizing and fit, which will vary according to the style of bike that the customer wants built. Steve describes his Bilenky Cycle Works as: " a happy, dirty place that turns out exquisitely clean machines to suit the needs of riders of every possible size, shape, and desire.

Ranging from pieces of "rideable jewelry" to utilitarian workhorses, each frame gives evidence to the Bilenky pursuit of aesthetic functionality."

In his other life, Steve is a bass guitarist alongside his fellow original members of the late-1970s band, the Notekillers. The discovery in 2003 that the band had been a formative influence on Sonic Youth—and by extension, the entire noise-rock revolution—led to the Notekillers reforming after a more than 20-year hiatus. The subsequent contact with Sonic Youth's Thurston Moore led to the re-release of the Notekillers' old recordings on Mr. Moore's own Ecstatic Peace label. New recordings and numerous gigs across the country soon followed, as well as an appearance at the All Tomorrow's Parties festival in England in 2006 and a European tour.

Steve has added son Aaron and daughter Bina to the Bilenky Cycle Works staff as computer-aided design technician and customer relations manager respectively. Somehow, the family still finds time for cyclo-tourism. The "FrameBuilder's Express" party train to NAHBS 2008 was one of the latest additions to the fun and adventure that makes up the world of Bilenky Cycle Works.

Bilenky cargo bike in Los Angeles

Rides like a dream ...

"Now that I've been riding my Bilenky for about six months (my daily commute and a couple of short tours have somehow totaled almost 3,000 miles), I can wholeheartedly say that I'm really happy with the bike. The mix of components we worked out together has been very reliable and cost-effective. The bike itself is not only beautiful but rides like a dream—of my three bikes it's certainly the most-ridden. I love how versatile this bike is and, unlike my other two bikes, I'm sure I'll still be riding my Bilenky ten years from now, if not longer. Yeah, the bike cost me some money, but when you think about how long I'm going to have it, I think it's actually working out to be a really good deal."

Thomas Delaney

Artisan Tourlite—753 tubing with stainless-steel lugs

Bina Bilenky's 26-inch-wheel Tourlite

Show frames from Cirque du Cyclisma 2007

Stephen fillet brazing dropouts

Fork finishing

Black Sheep Bikes

Fort Collins, Colorado USA

James Bleakley's quest to build custom bicycles comes from a driving passion to create something that evokes the feeling he had when riding bikes as an adolescent. The aesthetically pleasing curves from the 1920s, 30s, and 40s have inspired James to incorporate them into his bike designs. He likes to adapt contemporary geometry, handling, materials, and fabrication techniques to these kinds of older lines, which add a touch of elegance and evoke the spirit of the bike-building past.

The Ivor Johnson, some Schwinn designs, and a number of bikes that were built pre-WWII in the USA—where curves first started to appear in the cantilever style—the twin-top tubes, and the S bent-down tubes, have all provided inspiration to Black Sheep bike designs. Although the most efficient way to connect two points is a straight line, James believes that when another step like curving is added to the design it creates complexity: "The other thing you get from a curve, is compliance. When you're trying to compress a straight line that doesn't necessarily want to bend, if you introduce a curve, it automatically creates a way for there to be some compliance in the design."

James Bleakley wants to build his customers the last bike they will ever want to buy; something they can leave in their wills. Building a custom-fitted bike for someone takes into account many measurements of height, inseam, torso, and arm length, and the end result is designed to function in unison with the user's body: "Women particularly have a hard time buying a bike off the rack because very often what you're buying is a small man's bike, and a woman's body proportions are different."

James builds a number of bikes where the top tube has a negative curve so that it's a little easier to step through. Consideration is also given to where and how an individual is going to ride, the length of ride, the type of material the bike is going to be fabricated from, the shape, and of course the size. As an added feature, James likes to build peoples' own personal preferences and flair into the design. This may include a bottle opener on the bike's frame, for those times when you're out cycling and you feel like a beer.

Despite his busy design and building schedule, James still makes time to get out and ride. Riding provides his motivation and is a constant reminder as to why he builds bikes and loves doing it. The type of cycling that he like to do is ultra-endurance racing, such as the Leadville Trail 100 MTB in Leadville, Colorado, which climbs to 12,600 feet above sea level before descending back down to 10,000. It usually takes riders 8–11 hours to finish the race: "At the end of the day you don't even want to look at another bike!" However, the next day James can be found back in his workshop listening to talkback radio or music as he welds or bends another piece of titanium or steel to create a customer's dream bike.

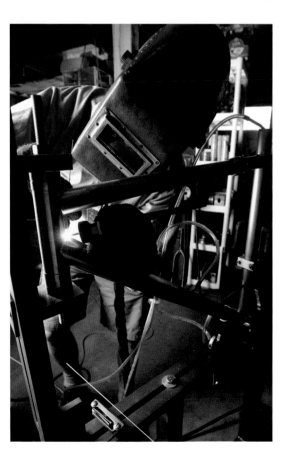

"When you're trying to compress a straight line that doesn't necessarily want to bend, if you introduce a curve, it automatically creates a way for there to be some compliance in the design."

Bob Brown Cycles

Saint Paul, Minnesota USA

The smooth, fluid lines of nature have provided inspiration for Bob Brown's lug carving and shoreline shapes during his past ten years of custom bike building. With nature supplying an infinite source of structures and shapes, Bob has far more ideas for designs than time will ever allow him to complete. Bob Brown builds exclusively with steel and stainless steel and likes to combine the classic look of a lugged frame with today's modern materials. His full stainless-steel frames are a great example of a traditional style executed with a very modern material.

Like many custom bike builders, Bob performs every aspect of the frame construction and design all the way though to the paint and assembly of a complete bike. Being a solo worker suits Bob because when he's building a frame so much of what is executed relies on the vision he has in his head. He describes himself as a tool junkie and his workspace is filled with a vast array of machinery and equipment, including some 50- to 60-year-old tools that were handed down from his grandfather. However, even with all the modern implements in the world he maintains that his most important tools are still his vise and files. Bob spends a lot of time hand filing each lug to create just the right curve or shape: "I put a lot of love into those parts and I think it shows in the final product."

The advantage of painting his own frames also allows Bob to design certain features of the frame to be painted in a specific way, creating a truly unique end product. An example of this is when he shapes stainless-steel lugs to ensure nice natural boundaries where the paint will stop at the lug edge or partway on the lug. Bob's favorite part of the whole building process is without a doubt brazing the frame: "I don't know why, but I love executing a really clean braze on a complicated part. Finishing off a braze with just the right amount of filler so that there are no voids and just a perfectly crisp lug shoreline is really rewarding."

When Bob isn't shaping, polishing, or painting a customer's unique frame, he's out riding bikes or cross-country skiing. He tries to run as many errands on his bike each day to keep active, satisfied that there's one less car on the road. He's also a sucker for ultra-endurance activity, so he tends to do a lot of really long rides, runs, and skiing sessions.

Bob loves to share his passions with others and has been known to coach high school ski teams for fun during the winter season. If you're out enjoying some local music in Saint Paul, Minnesota, you may also spot Bob playing drums in a local band called Derailleur, which has also been another lifelong activity. Bob Brown likes to do anything but sit still.

Dragonfly lug with copper-plated finish

"I don't know why, but I love executing a really clean braze on a complicated part. Finishing off a braze with just the right amount of filler so that there are no voids and just a perfectly crisp lug shoreline is really rewarding."

Complete sport-touring road bike

Polished stainless-steel lugged bicycle

Brazing a fork in the jig

"I put a lot of love into those parts and I think it shows in the final product."

Seat lug detail, polished stainless lug

My bike was built to change my life …

"Because my bike was built for me, it looks exactly like I want it to, handles exactly like I had always hoped a bike would, and, literally, has saved my life. Bikes may be just bikes to some, but not to me. My bike was built to change my life. Starting back in late 2005, at 501 pounds, I had only one way out … or die. My way out was to ride a bike that was built for me. I'm currently down to 219 pounds—my bike has saved my life. In the process, my bike gave me more freedom, enjoyment, interaction, insight, and revelation than nearly any other single thing in my lifetime. If those aren't all great reasons to love your bike, I sincerely don't know what is. Bob Brown built my bike, and I ride that bike every single day."

Scott Cutshall

Bohemian Bicycles

Tucson, Arizona USA

Dave Bohm knew from a very early age that he wanted to design some kind of transport; he was car and motorcycle crazy and after discovering bicycles he realised that, at the time, they were much more accessible to him. Dave believes that bikes are much more than a machine—they are also art in a usable format. He considers himself very fortunate to have been exposed to paintings, sculptures, buildings, and automobiles at a very young age and holds the belief that his handcrafted bicycles are objects truly created from his mind as well as his hands.

The type of material from which a bike is made is inconsequential to Dave because he believes great bicycles can be made from a multitude of materials like bamboo, metals, or carbons. The most important thing to him is how particular materials are utilized and how they either allow or disallow creativity in design and form. For various reasons he has chosen to work exclusively in steel for its almost unlimited design flexibility and because it's a very forgiving medium. Composite materials promise the same type of freedom, but Dave feels that working with steel best utilizes his skills: "There are many excellent bicycles made from other materials, but in this area

I excel so I stick with it." Dave predominately works alone, but has recently taken on an apprentice helper who frees up his time to concentrate on the more detailed and creative work, which is the hallmark of Bohemian Bicycles.

Unlike many other frame builders, Dave's background is in precious metal-works as a silversmith, and therefore he brings a skill set to his work that is rarely seen in the industry. While first and foremost the bicycles must perform the task for which they've been designed, Dave considers detailing as the icing on the cake and enjoys the lug preparation and paint stages the most: "To that end I incorporate non-traditional lug cutting, accoutrement in precious metals, original stainless dropouts, nameplates, themes, and paint that are all completed to the highest caliber."

Many of Dave's customers have been riders for some time and through interviews and the reviewing of various pictures and designs, they come up with a riding position and design together. Apart from the usual measurements, fitness level, flexibility, and intended riding purpose are all extremely important factors in the fitting process. A large number of

Dave's customers have become good friends and continue to email him with their travel stories and pictures of their Bohemian bikes.

One of the most rewarding aspects of his business is that each customer brings a unique background and purpose to the bike building process. For example, Dave was given the opportunity to design and construct a unique tricycle for Noel Kreidler, who has Muscular Dystrophy: "Noel came to me because although she has limited use of her lower limbs the cycling motion was something she could do to maintain lower body strength. Her old tricycle was extremely heavy and had limited gears, meaning any hills whatsoever were out of the question—the design of her new trike enables her to tackle hills as well as cruising on the flat. Noel's tricycle features a very low stand over height with a wide, open mounting platform that enables her to mount the trike much more easily; it also includes a parking brake so that the trike remains stable while moving from a chair or walker. I'm glad Noel gave me the opportunity to be creative and to find a solution that will keep her healthier, longer—it simply reinforces the fact that pedaled vehicles are therapeutic as well as fun."

Rohloff touring bike frame

"I incorporate non-traditional lug cutting, accoutrement in precious metals, original stainless dropouts, nameplates, themes, and paint that are all completed to the highest caliber."

Bohemian Orange Crush 29nr

My trusted companion ...

"I never considered taking any bike but my faithful Bohemian to the Pyrenees. Dave builds beautiful and functional bikes, and mine had been my trusted companion for over 55,000 miles, including the Cochise Classic 250, the Death Ride, several bike tours of Colorado and El tours, and about a hundred trips up (and down) Mt. Lemmon in Tucson, Arizona. The bike is comfortable on long rides, steady as a rock on descents, and no other bike would do for a once-in-a-lifetime trip like the Pyrenean Raid, more than 400 miles of epic climbs in four days."

Rupert Laumann

This tricycle was custom-built for Noel Kreidler

Bruce Gordon Cycles

Petaluma, California USA

Bruce Gordon is a highly regarded master frame builder with 33 years of experience behind him. Bruce has a similar background to many other experienced bike builders—he worked in a bike shop at a young age, was into cycling, and got hooked on the idea of making his own bikes. The bicycle that Bruce Gordon is particularly known for is his touring bike, which is deemed by many touring aficionados in the United States as one of the best touring bikes around. Today, the vast majority of Bruce's work consists of TIG-welded steel touring bikes, although his real creative expression is evident in his steel-lugged bikes, which he built for the first 12 years of his building career. Bruce has returned to building these bikes because of the depth of detail and creative expression that can be achieved.

The traditions of frame building and levels of craftsmanship are evident when ordering a custom-made bike from a frame builder with so much experience and expertise as Bruce Gordon. His skill levels are such that he has built a one-off, lugged-titanium bike that no one else would come near to producing. As much of Bruce's reputation is built on his touring bikes, particularly his Rock 'n Road model, many people seek him out to get their dream touring bike constructed for that special trip that they've been intending to make for years. Many of Bruce's customers range from people in their 70s who want to tour the world, through to younger riders who are discovering a love for touring.

When designing a touring bike for someone, it's imperative to Bruce that there is appropriate geometry and tubing and well-positioned rack mounts that cater to the specific purpose of touring bikes. His aim is to figure out how he can make a bike for touring that will function better than anything else that is out on the road or currently available. In recent years, Bruce has been turning his design skills toward many innovative ideas and has created new custom bike part designs out of titanium. The designs are reminiscent of the French style and his range of aesthetically crafted accessories include front and rear panniers, racks, CNC'd milled rear lights and cantilever brakes, toe clips, pumps, and seat posts. Bruce Gordon is always trying to stretch the design boundaries with his bicycles in order to create a point of difference.

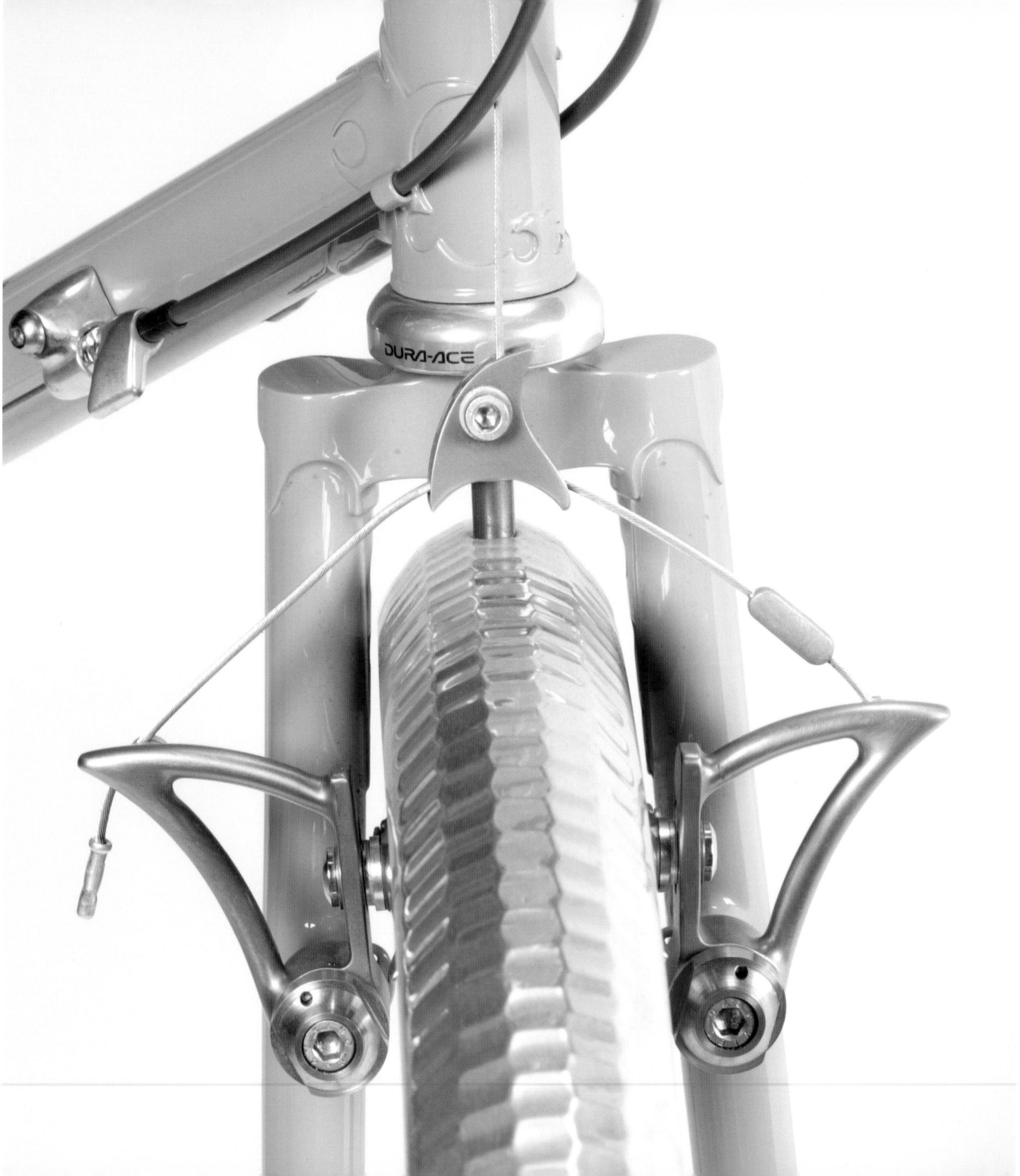
DURA-ACE

Calfee Design

La Selva Beach, California USA

Well before mountain bikes were invented, Craig Calfee was one of those kids who took his regular bike into the woods, and in doing so joined a generation of young trailblazers that helped to create the concept of mountain bikes. During his college years, Craig graduated to riding bikes in New York City as a bike messenger, and when his bike was damaged he discovered an interest in its structure. Although he was an arts student majoring in sculpture, it was at this point that Craig began to think about bikes as industrial design.

At the time, he was working at a carbon fiber boat building company and used the materials he was working with and his own techniques to build himself a new bike. This first bike didn't fit him very well, so he decided to learn more about the technical aspects of bike construction. By borrowing a friend's Massachusetts Institute of Technology library card, Craig read everything he could get his hands on and sought out advice from other frame builders. He then moved to California and began building carbon-fiber frames in his San Francisco garage. Three-time Tour de France-winner Greg LeMond discovered Craig's

bikes in 1991. The thrill of seeing Greg wearing the yellow jersey, riding a bike that he had made, provided the inspiration for Craig to delve deeper into the possibilities of bicycle design.

Craig had always been interested in trying out new things and playing with unorthodox materials, and in 1998 he started building bikes out of bamboo for family and friends. His bamboo bikes were such a success that in 2006 Calfee Design began producing them for the general public. Craig believes bamboo offers even more opportunities to customize than carbon fiber because the bamboo tubes allow for an infinite variety of naturally formed diameters and wall thicknesses with which to work. Bamboo also provides natural butting because the cane grows a thick wall at its base and the wall thickness tapers as it grows. Calfee bike designs are very much embedded in nature and the notion that form follows function.

Calfee Design has also extended its bamboo bike-building philosophy and skills to help people in Africa build bikes. Many years ago, Craig traveled through Africa and learned that bamboo was a plentiful resource and that people were very resourceful and skilled with their hands. In June 2007, he went to Ghana on an Earth Institute-funded feasibility study to investigate the viability of local production of bamboo bikes. As it turned out, there was keen interest in projects that are self-sustaining and add value to communities' skills and economies. Craig regularly returns to Ghana to continue helping the community develop their skills. Back in California, the 15-member team at Calfee are fortunate to work in a beautiful beachside location near Santa Cruz, where there is plenty of good light and ventilation plus views of agricultural fields. "You really can't ask for a better location. It's very aesthetically pleasing and close to nature."

Columbine Cycle Works

Mendocino, California USA

Established in 1979, Columbine Cycle Works had its genesis in the childhood years of the Murphy brothers. John and Richard were making and fixing things such as bikes and soapbox cars, and were fed a steady diet of powered model airplanes, boats, and cars from as early as they can remember. Light racing bikes became their next area of interest, inspired by Richard's job at a Denver pro bike shop in the early 1970s. This sparked an interest in frame building and by 1979 they registered the name Columbine after a period of time building, repairing, and repainting frames.

Establishing Columbine was a natural progression for John and Richard as they have always shared the same core value that bicycle making epitomizes: that simplicity and beauty can elevate a simple machine to an art form. "It is a complete passion with social, athletic, technical, and aesthetic dimensions." A hallmark of John and Richard's frame building has always been to try to find a way to build the lightest frames available. They believe the weight of a frame is the fundamental ingredient

to making a first-rate riding bike, and that comfort and longer life expectancy are engineered by controlling the spring-like movement of the tubes. John's background in structural physics has allowed him to assimilate those ideas while developing the lightweight methodology. He prefers to work with steel or stainless steel because both metals have a very good modulus of elasticity, along with other specific properties, with which to build the perfect unbreakable spring. According to John, "Steel makes bikes that 'sing' to you!"

There are many features on a bike that John Murphy admires, but he's particularly fascinated by the sparkle of a really light set of stainless tension-spoked wheels on a running bike, which he describes as a mechanical marvel that's nothing short of miraculous. When it comes to frame features, he usually finds himself checking out the seat stay cluster for geometric delights, or there's always the well-done rear dropout joint for its expression of creativity.

Columbine bikes are well known for the intricate accoutrements, elegant lugs, and paintwork that adorn them, elevating them to moving works of art. Although they build bikes that provide a metal canvas for exquisite creative expression, the philosophy and challenge that really underpins John and Richard Murphy's ultimate goal is to make ultra-light frames that will ride like a dream.

"It is a complete passion with social, athletic, technical, and aesthetic dimensions."

Crisp Titanium

Arezzo, Italy

Darren Mark Crisp can still describe his first two-wheeler bike in great detail. Those two wheels gave him a sense of freedom and movement, but the future bike builder was already wanting to trim the seat stays back to make his AMF Roadmaster look more like the slick Schwinn Scrambler BMX bikes that all the cool neighborhood kids were riding. For a boy who grew up in the United States, there seems to be a certain synergy and logical progression to how Darren finally ended up designing and building bikes in Italy out of his material of choice, titanium.

His take on bike design was very much influenced by seven years of project management work in the construction industry. Overseeing the building of exclusive, high-end retail stores from materials such as stainless steel, nickel steel, nickel silver, and titanium gave Darren the opportunity to use some of the finest tooling equipment, do lots of welding, and liaise with the top engineering and fabrication minds alongside elite designers and architects. This period of his life very much influenced his take on bicycle design and his approach to building—clean lines, no frills, form follows function, high-tech—and also his desire to build a better product.

When Darren first started building bikes, he was using True Temper steel and Henry James lugs for much of his work, though he also experimented with other materials such as aluminum and scandium. In 2001 he attended the United Bicycle Institute to study titanium frame design, which effectively sealed the deal on his choice of metal for bicycle frame building. Darren's studio is located in Tuscany, where he lives with his family in a villa surrounded by vineyards, olive groves, and a scenic view of the walled town of Castiglion Fiorentino. While music usually provides a relaxing backdrop to Darren's working day, in spring and summer he prefers the comforting sounds of live music provided by the merli (blackbirds) in the early evening and the sound of his family talking and playing in the adjacent yard.

Darren performs all the design development, cutting, welding, and finishing work. Welding, however, is his favorite part of the building process, which he finds particularly stimulating for various reasons: the challenge of laying the perfect bead, the rhythm that is both relaxing and exciting, the technical aspects of the sterile weld, and the mechanics of fusing titanium tubes together and looking at a freshly finished welded frame knowing that it's only days away from being on a road or trail in some faraway place. Aside from the overall form and design of a bike, which is his first priority, he likes dropouts because they are very revealing. They can divulge where the builder is from, the design intent behind the bike, and the taste of the cyclist: "I don't think there is any one aspect of a frame that tells more of a story than the drops."

His decision to work exclusively with titanium is strongly based on his experience in the metals industry and from learning early on that making the best products requires having complete understanding of your building materials. Darren chose titanium because of his direct working experience, along with its magnificent ride qualities. He believes it is a superb material for building bike frames because it is corrosion resistant, provides a supple ride, is lightweight, and has the mechanical strength needed to build a frame for a lifetime: "One can update components on a yearly basis, but the elegant look of a custom titanium frame is timeless."

Head tube/fork detail

Apart from the sheer beauty …

"I think the most gratifying aspect of a custom-made frame is the knowledge that it has been made for me. Not some standardized model of me, but the real me with all the physical quirks nature has given me. If you add titanium into the equation, with all its durability, ride quality, and so on, then you are getting close to perfection. While there are plenty of gorgeous bikes out there (and I have no objection to carbon fiber itself), now I've got a bike that rides great and is going to last forever, and I actually know the guy who created it. Hard to beat."

Brendan Jones, Rome Italy

Crisp custom titanium road bike

Crisp custom titanium 29er

Detail of rear triangle

Seat tube/top tube detail

Crisp demonstrates welding types

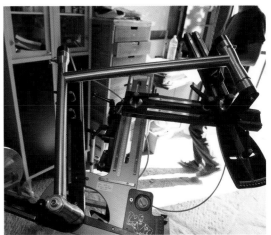

Tacking fixture

"I don't think there is any one aspect of a frame that tells more of a story than the drops."

Amadeo Bonfanti competing on a Crisp

Veneto champion Dionisi heads toward victory

"One can update components on a yearly basis, but the elegant look of a custom titanium frame is timeless."

Cycles Alex Singer

Levallois-Perret, Paris France

Stepping over the shop threshold of 53 rue Victor Hugo, it is immediately evident that this is a cycling shop steeped in history. The wooden cash register on the counter and the many vintage cycling photos adorning the walls recall a cycling era that people are rediscovering. There is also a range of new and historic bikes on display, including a tandem bicycle on which frame builder Olivier Csuka's mother and father raced. The bike is so well made and immaculately kept that it looks like it was made yesterday. Established by Alex Singer almost 70 years ago, the Cycles Alex Singer was successfully operated for 50 years by Ernest Csuka, with the help of his wife, Leone, and his brother, Roland. The family business is still producing finely crafted bicycles and is run by Olivier Csuka, Ernest's son.

Ernest, who only recently retired from frame building, served a lengthy apprenticeship alongside Alex and took over the reins a few years before Alex Singer died in 1966. Alex, who was born in Hungary and came to France in 1919, was an excellent randonneur cyclist and the winner of many concours de machines, and in later years he was also a competitive racing cyclist. When he ended his cycling career, Alex decided that he wanted to create his own bicycles. Levallois-Perret in the 1940s was the capital of handmade cars and also supported an aviation industry, so there were many men in the region with exceptional hand and fabricating skills. As there was no recognized bicycle building industry at the time, the only way to acquire a bicycle was to either make it yourself or approach the growing number of people who could build one for you. In order to make extra money, many men from Levallois-Perret used their skills to construct bicycle frames, and it was in this environment that Alex Singer developed his frame-building skills.

At the time, there were no factory-made bicycle parts so the builders had to create their own designs and models and build most parts from scratch. Consequently, much technical innovation occurred as the frame builders were forced to be inventive with their construction and designs. Through sheer ingenuity and resourcefulness, these men handproduced parts such as derailers, stands, seat posts, cranks, fenders, and all manner of elements used in the production of a functional bicycle. According to Olivier Csuka, Alex Singer was an exceptionally creative man and worked by himself until Olivier's father Ernest and his uncle became apprentices to him in 1944. Olivier was just a young boy when Alex passed away, but he remembers him as a happy and reserved man and was lucky enough to have spent many hours in the workshop observing and learning the art of fabrication from his father.

Having grown up around bike building, observing Alex and learning the art of fabrication from his father, Olivier believes he has responsibility to carry on the family tradition of bike building. Although Olivier is involved in other work outside of Cycles Alex Singer, he still continues to build mainly touring bikes in the Alex Singer tradition, while also restoring original Singer bicycles. Olivier is a keen road and track racer and has won a number of championships in his 30 years of competition. The main priority for Olivier is that his bikes are well crafted and that they are fitted correctly for the bike's purpose. Longtime customer Yannick chose Alex Singer Cycles for its reputation for making the finest bikes. Yannick owns two Singer bikes, a racer, and a randonneur, and recognizes that having a hand-built, custom bike made was an investment in cycling for life.

Cyfac

La Fuye, Indre et Loire France

Cyfac's founder, Francis Quillon, opened the doors of his first workshop in France's Touraine region in 1982. As a former racer and team frame builder, he was confident in his quest for technological and sporting advancement. Quillon focused on craftsmanship and the latest innovations to deliver high-quality, cutting-edge products. Today, the Cyfac employees, led by Executive Manager Aymeric Le Brun, continue Francis's passion for custom-made frames through the design elements, materials, and techniques that are expressed in their handmade craftsmanship and finish. "We have an *orfevre* finish, which approaches near perfection with the presence of an invisible weld line on our aluminum frames and flawless tube junctions on our carbon models."

Cyfac builds its bikes from a range of materials and appreciates each for different reasons. Steel is firmly embedded into the beginning of Cyfac's 25-year history and has advantages with respect to comfort and the ability to be repaired anywhere in the world. Cyfac claim to have produced some of the first alloy frames and the first builder to master the TIG welding of aluminum. Alloy is appreciated for its reactivity, the quality of the welds, and lightness of frames; Cyfac built the first alloy frames that were raced in the Tour de France. When it comes to building with carbon, the Cyfac team feels that it can produce whatever a customer wishes because there are so many possibilities. The frame can be made stiff or flexible, with a carbon finish or a paint finish; importantly, the carbon frames are light, comfortable, and durable. Cyfac also combines the two "noble" materials of titanium and carbon to build a traditional but very high-tech frame that pairs the natural comfort of titanium with the road filtration and stiffness of carbon.

For Aymeric Le Brun, managing Cyfac provides a constant sense of excitement because his work differs from day to day and because the range of skills executed by the work team is world-class. "For carbon frames, the wrapping process is the most interesting, but for all the frames, the painting process is the most inspiring because it requires precision, patience, and skill." When fitting customers for a new bike, Cyfac has developed its own system, referred to as the Cyfac Postural System. It allows Cyfac to optimize rider comfort, performance, and health by following very stringent and well-tested criteria for performance. People who order a custom bike not only want to have a bike that perfectly fits their body, but they also want to own something that is unique. Some customers will ask Cyfac to paint their name on the down tube where the name Cyfac normally appears, while others have traveled from abroad to visit the workshop so they can personally choose the frame color.

At the end of each day Aymeric likes to look at the wonderful frames that have been produced, take some photos to send to customers who are anxiously awaiting their new Cyfac bicycle, and weather allowing, he rides his bicycle home, which makes it a perfect day.

Cyfacs look fast just sitting still

"For carbon frames, the wrapping process is the most interesting, but for all the frames, the painting process is the most inspiring because it requires precision, patience, and skill."

Cyfac's CADENCE frameset features the ultra comfortable, high-performance DoubleStay2 rear triangle

Cyfac's custom GOTHICA; 14,000 possible paint tints yield unique custom creations

Cyfac's CADENCE line-up

"We have an orfevre finish, which approaches near perfection with the presence of an invisible weld line on our aluminum frames and flawless tube junctions on our carbon models."

Davidson Handbuilt Bicycles

Seattle, Washington USA

Bill Davidson was a young, impressionable fellow in the early 1970s when the United States was experiencing a bike boom. At the time, Bill was into running but had friends who were into cycling, so decided he would give "this cycling thing" a go. Cycle racing was hugely popular in British Columbia, which was only three hours from Seattle, and Bill would head there with his cycling friends most weekends for some road racing. The European cycling heritage and influence was much stronger in Canada, and Bill admits that he and his friends didn't have much of a clue and were "shredded" every weekend by the better-trained and tactical Canadian riders.

Although cycling was bigger than baseball at the turn of the 20th century in the United States, the advent of the car and improved public transport meant that interest in cycling gradually fell away. Bill's father had established a welding shop in Seattle after WWII that fabricated all sorts of mechanical parts, so Bill spent much of his youth surrounded by machining, welding, and painting. When he started building bikes, it was a one-man operation, so he was involved in every single step of the process.

Bill would measure the customer, design the frame, purchase the componentry, paint the frame, install the componentry, fit the customer to the bike, and finally sit back and watch as each proud owner rode off with a new hand-built Davidson bicycle. During that process, there were also several other bikes waiting for Bill to work on, all at different stages of production.

Seven hundred frames later, Bill realized that, "It was going to be a tough road to hoe to do business this way," and decided that he needed to focus his experience and expertise where it was most needed. He realized that his skills would be best served in fitting the customer, helping them arrive at the ideal bike, and specifying the right components, so he employed specialized staff to assist him in his workshop. Davidson bikes are built from beginning to end under the one roof at Bill's workshop in Elliott Bay, Seattle; this way, Bill is able maintain his high production standards and supervise the entire process. He's also constantly looking for new and interesting ways of producing his bikes, which is why he builds with titanium and carbon fiber in addition to more traditional materials and methods.

As a master builder with 35 years of experience behind him, Bill is committed to helping young people who are open-minded, eager, and show aptitude for frame building. Bill mentors this next generation of bike builders at his workshop, where he likes to foster the pride that one gets from executing specific skills in the best possible way. He also has a philosophy of empowering the people that work with him and encourages them to come up with new ideas and innovations for Davidson bikes.

Don Walker Cycles

Speedway, Indiana USA

As the founder of the North American Handmade Bike Show, Don Walker has been the driving force behind more than 100 custom bike builders gathering annually to showcase their craftsmanship. Don believes that people are gradually discovering the benefits of owning a custom-made bike because it offers them the opportunity to own a bike that fits them exactly and is an expression of their individuality. He believes that owners of custom-made bikes are saying, "Maybe I don't want to be the guy that keeps showing up for the Saturday morning ride looking like every one else." Don also believes that people are presently rediscovering the joy of getting out in the open air and feeling the rush of wind on their face and through their hair.

Don Walker's passion for cycling was awakened around the age of 14, when everyone in his neighborhood started buying road bikes and going on 25- to 35-mile rides. When he got a bike, he found that his real passion was for track racing and competed in the sport through his high school years. Don loves track racing because of the certain energy that emanates from a velodrome when the riders are battling it out on the track and the spectators

are cheering them on. In his racing days, Don was always ready to do battle on the track and when he discovered 10 years ago that his surname was connected to a Scottish clan who used to paint their naked bodies blue and run screaming toward their opponents wielding battleaxes and claymores, it went some way to explaining his approach to track cycling. Proud of his Scottish heritage, many of Don's bikes feature tartan paint designs and the decal on each head stem features a tartan background—castle peaks around the shield and two crossed claymores.

Don's bike-building skills were developed over many years while working as an aircraft mechanic. With a passion for track bikes and the skill set to build them, he began producing bikes in California in the 1990s. Don is now based in Indianapolis and builds a range of bike models including tandems, but track bikes are still his number one love.

When a customer comes to Don to be fitted for a bike, he likes to go for a ride with his client to see where they are in relation to the bike. This method means that he can build a more complete picture of the rider's physique and riding style as well as taking

the usual measurements. Like so many bike builders who have been building and observing riders for years, Don can usually figure out people's measurements in the first couple of minutes by just looking at them.

Don Walker also likes to include his sense of humor into some of this paint designs. On one of his tandem track bikes, which he refers to as "the tandem of death," the crime scene yellow tape painted on the top tube says: "Crime Scene Do Not Cross." The boom tube that runs between the front and rear bottom bracket features a sidewalk scene with blood and chalk outlines of bodies. "It's a track tandem, they're very dangerous, and not everyone should be riding one. It's like I've got to make it as morbid as I can because if I don't beat somebody on the track, at least I want them to fear me!"

"Maybe I don't want to be the guy that keeps showing up for the Saturday morning ride looking like every one else."

GURU Bicycles

Montreal, Québec Canada

As an engineering student, cycling fan, and bike aficionado, Tony Giannascoli decided in the mid 1990s to build himself a bike from scratch. He was always taking bikes apart and putting them back together, but couldn't resist adding an extra element in the process. Tony began getting requests from people who admired his bike and from the outset he wanted to custom build in order to get the perfect fit for optimizing performance. Tony's father is a tailor, so he understands the tradition behind making a bespoke garment for someone. He quickly found that he was doing things a little differently from the rest of the industry by leaning on his engineering background and finding inspiration from the world of aeronautics to push things forward: "I'm a scientist at heart, so being progressive with materials and methods used is essential for me."

The team of 30 Guru workers produces a range of custom bikes made from carbon, aluminum, titanium, and steel, with each material possessing its own inherent qualities and characteristics. Tony believes that carbon allows for the creation of the most favorable shapes to deliver optimal stiffness for aerodynamics and ride quality. Building seamless, custom carbon bikes at Guru is a particular technical challenge and rewarding process. On the other hand, Tony knows there's nothing quite like a beautiful titanium weld and those who ride titanium swear by it.

The Guru team works to the sound of tubes being milled and bikes being buffed as carbon lay-up process specialists, welders, pre-prep, and paint and clear coating workers go about their daily business. They aim to create a bike that perfectly fits the individual by ensuring that the critical interface between rider and bicycle is set up to achieve optimal power transfer, aerodynamics, and overall ride quality. In terms of the benefits, their customers say that once you have ridden a good custom bike there's no going back. A testament to people's passion for riding on a bicycle they love is an 80-year-old Guru customer whose husband follows her every pedal stroke in his car to protect her while she's riding. Jeannine still manages to ride more than 1200 miles every summer.

The attention to detail that goes into customizing a Guru bike is evident in all components, right down to the head badge. The crest containing the logo features a series of dots representing a cross section of stacked tubes. When one of the tubes is selected for a bike, the right dot on the second row is painted in the same color as the logo, which leaves a capital G in the background. Each head badge is hand-painted to match the client's chosen color scheme, representing Guru's commitment to making bikes one detail at a time. "When you can deliver cutting-edge bikes that are also beautifully handcrafted for one particular person, you're making something special. Honoring those two masters, science and art, is an ongoing challenge for us."

Opposite: Guru Geneo, road bicycle

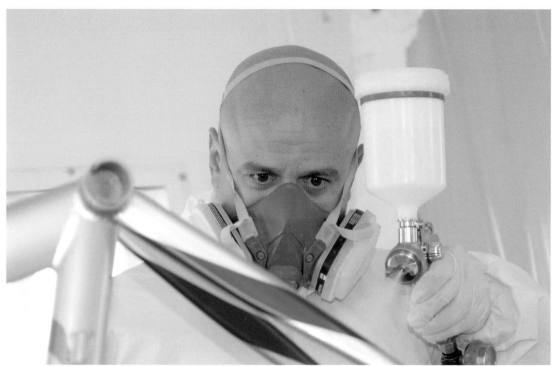

"I'm a scientist at heart, so being progressive with materials and methods used is essential for me."

Trained hands and eyes apply a finishing clear coat

The Guru factory, located in Montreal, Canada

Premium-grade carbon fiber is precisely cut based on individual specifications

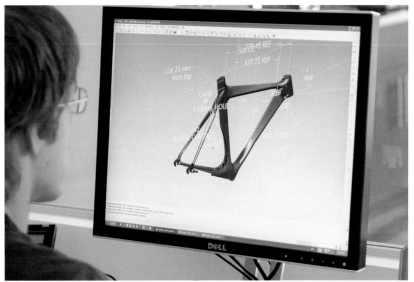

One of Guru's engineers oversees the generation of a custom bike design

Guru's hand-painted head badge (The One) is applied as a crowning jewel

"When you can deliver cutting-edge bikes that are also beautifully handcrafted for one particular person, you're making something special. Honoring those two masters, science and art, is an ongoing challenge for us."

Titanium welded à la Guru

The best bike I have ridden ...

"When you buy a bike, you think of quite a few different things: the material it's made of, the reputation of the manufacturer, the way it rides, and to be honest, the way it looks. When I bought my Guru Crono from Jack and Adam's in Austin, I spent five hours trying different bikes, different wheel sets, and fiddling with adjustments to get the bikes as close as I could in all ways except the frame. I settled on the Crono because it was, quite simply, the best bike I have ridden in 30 years of riding, including seasons of bike racing and six Ironman Triathlons. It accelerated, it was soft and smooth, it was so responsive. Had someone tried to tell me this in advance, I wouldn't have believed them. But when I rode it, I found myself smiling and shaking my head—truly, I did—on a back road of Austin, because I just didn't know a bike could feel like that."
Peter Stevens

Guru Crono, triathlon / carbon TT Bicycle

Independent Fabrication

Somerville, Massachusetts USA

The diversity of skills and overall teamwork of the 13 members of Independent Fabrication give the company great depth and make the bicycles they produce inherently special. The team regards its bike building as a career and each individual at Independent Fabrication comes from extremely different backgrounds. For some, bike building is a mechanical and sculptural outlet, and for others it's more about the technical aspects, but for all of Independent Fabrication's employees it is an opportunity to interact with like-minded individuals who are joined by a common task.

Being a group of highly critical, proud, and creative individuals also helps to push the Independent Fabrication team to make the best bicycles they can. Most of the team are cross-trained, which enables individuals to work in multiple departments, and at any given time they can find themselves welding a steel, titanium, or stainless-steel frame. Materials are the essence of each frame because the variety of materials at their disposal ensures that they can dial in the "feel" of a bike that specifically relates to the customer.

The Independent Fabrication team believes that their building methods provide the greatest amount of flexibility in terms of geometry, tube selection, and quality. The variety of jobs and materials used keeps everyone in the team on their toes and pushes everyone to improve their skills every day. "Our bikes are distinctive because of the who, the where, and the how. We feel that the end results speak for themselves. The custom nature of our product, coupled with the vast array of material choices and frame options, make our frames and our company appealing to all types of bicycles lovers."

The love of cycling and passion for bikes extends to most of the team commuting by bike to work each day, and during the summer months many of them also ride mountain and road bikes for reasons other than mere transportation. When the crew at Independent Fabrication aren't honing their skills at work or on their bikes, they can be found working on houses, making furniture and store display fixtures, taking care of children, climbing mountains, conquering skate parks, and generally enjoying life to the full.

Titanium Deluxe

Sterling silver head badge

TIG welding a steel frame

"Our bikes are distinctive because of the who, the where, and the how. We feel that the end results speak for themselves. The custom nature of our product coupled with the vast array of material choices and frame options make our frames and our company appealing to all types of bicycles lovers."

Painting a fork

Final machining process

Stainless-steel road bike

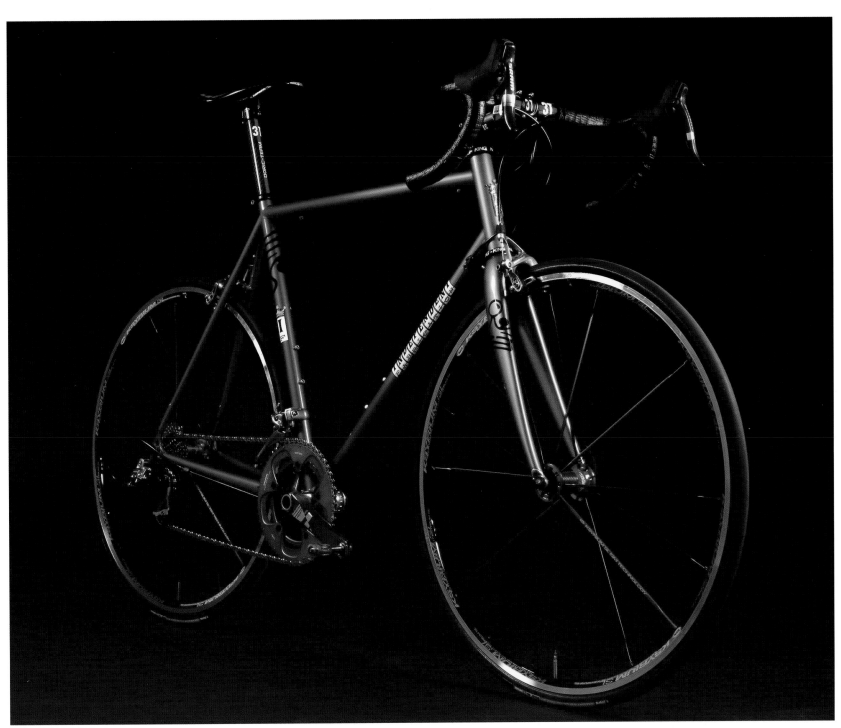

Factory Lightweight

Ira Ryan Cycles

Portland, Oregon USA

One hundred percent pure riding is the passion that carries Ira Ryan to his workshop each day to hand build his custom bicycles. He has never fitted into one particular category, but describes himself as a cyclist, not a cycling enthusiast. "Anybody on two wheels, as far as I'm concerned, is a friend." He found working as a bicycle mechanic for 12 years, using tools and fixing bikes, a very gratifying experience and considers his hands to be his most important assets.

An adherence to the simplicity of using his hands and minimal tools to create something wonderful is evident in the way Ira works. When designing a bicycle for a customer there are no computers involved and no complex calculations, however there is a lot of talking and he likes to draw everything on paper in full size. For the first year and a half of Ira Ryan Cycles, he didn't even have a milling machine, so all the production was done with a hacksaw, files, and sandpaper. Being a bike mechanic and having ridden motorcycles made Ira realize how much specific finessing of design goes into making a custom bicycle. It also made him appreciate the utilitarian nature of bicycles, and the ability to repair them on the side of the road with a minimal amount of equipment.

"Each frame is a step toward an understanding of a craft that takes a lifetime to master and remains difficult to perfect."

When establishing his business it wasn't just the bikes that were paramount—Ira also needed to think about his brand. He made several lists of potential names, but none really stuck, so he settled for Ira Ryan Cycles: "It's your name, it's your bike." At first he found it weird to hear people talk about Ira Ryan as a bike instead of Ira Ryan the person, but having heard it since 2005 he's now used to it. For his head badge, Ira decided to use the image of a swallow. He grew up on a small farm in America's Midwest where the barn swallows would come every summer. The swallow evoked memories of cycle touring and racing in the Midwest — flying down the road on a bike and suddenly riding into a swarm of swallows. It was watching them move and carve the wind that made Ira realize that's what it felt like to ride a bike.

During his time as a bike mechanic, one memory stands out as the first time he experienced the intense feeling of satisfaction from a day's work using your hands and having something to show for it at the end. "It was the face of a child whose training wheels were removed for the first time. It was that feeling of being totally alive, the feeling of freedom, that first exhilarating experience on a bicycle." Ira wants to be part of the next step in bike building that pushes the boundaries of what is being created today, but is also able to appreciate the beauty of what has been made before. His bicycles are about remembering the roads you have ridden in the past, feeling the experience of those moments, and also looking forward to the many miles of road that you will ride in a lifetime.

"Each frame is a step toward an understanding of a craft that takes a lifetime to master and remains difficult to perfect."

"Anybody on two wheels, as far as I'm concerned, is a friend."

Jeff Jones Custom Bicycles

Medford, Oregon USA

Jeff Jones has a very simple philosophy: "I love to ride bikes and I want to build a bike the way I want it." In his desire to build bikes he truly believes in, Jeff has gone against the normal trend of putting suspension on his mountain bikes. He's into performance riding and prefers to do it without suspension. Therefore, he builds high-performance, non-suspension bicycles built for function, not for fashion, regardless of how it has been done in the past, what the tradition says, and what "looks" right. Consequently, Jeff has a high regard for developing bikes using simple logic and design.

He believes that the rideability of his bikes is enhanced because the rider isn't isolated from the ground and what's going on beneath them. In a pure sense, the rider is riding a bicycle, not a bicycle with a whole lot of extra things bolted to it to make the trail feel like it's no longer there. His bikes teach the rider to pick a line down the trail and to feel the ground. You can hop it, you can hit the brakes and the bike doesn't dive, it doesn't rock and it takes it back to the beautiful, pure bicycle, which is a couple of wheels, a steering head, a crank, and a chain. Jeff's commitment to his frame designs and riding

style has come from many years of riding and racing down hills, hopping and jumping over things on his front wheel, plus many years of working in bike shops.

When Jeff tells a customer that his bikes are capable of doing particular manoeuvers, they can be confident in this knowledge because he's always out on the trails putting his bikes through their paces. Knowing what his bikes are capable of is only part of the picture when working with a customer, so he puts a lot of time into finding out exactly what he's going to build for someone. Jeff prefers to get out and ride with someone to watch their riding style so he can pick out strengths and weaknesses. If this process isn't possible, he likes customers to send him a video of them riding. He also asks lots of questions about riding style, riding history, and performance. He believes in having lots of stand-over height, and a frame that flexes vertically as much as it can. He takes inspiration for the design of his forks from cranes, bridges and early motorcycles, and the flexible frame is based on the flex of airplane wings.

Making the bike work for riding is his only priority and if people think his bikes are also beautiful, that's fine. The only purely aesthetic feature on his bikes is the head badge, which features the mountain behind his house with the wheel in the middle. It was designed by Jeff in conjunction with an artist and crafted by a jeweler. Jeff's workspace is under his house, located up in the woods away from everything. This location helps to keep his mind uncluttered and allows him to be hauled off in his own direction without being pushed back in line with how everyone else is building mountain bikes. He particularly likes working at night when no one else is around and will sometimes get into a 20-hour roll and just keep going, crashing out for the next day and then getting back into it again: "It's about the flow of how things are going—you stay in there and you don't have to think about it too much, it just comes out."

Truss fork detail

Why do I love my bike?

"It might be the design and craftsmanship—the unique combination of insight and engineering. It could be the obvious attention to every single detail. I must say I don't love it for its looks—when form follows function you don't get conventional beauty. No, I love my bike because it makes me happy, it makes me smile. There's not been one ride in the years I've had it when it hasn't inspired me and impressed me with its capabilities and appropriateness. There hasn't been one ride when I haven't had my spirits lifted. I'm not one for angles or tubing profiles but I love riding a bike that feels and reacts like it is a part of me."

Anonymous

"I love to ride bikes and I want to build a bike the way I want it … It's about the flow of how things are going—you stay in there and you don't have to think about it too much, it just comes out."

Keith Anderson Cycles

Grants Pass, Oregon USA

As a child, bicycles gave Keith his first taste of freedom and he's been in love with them ever since. When he was a young man he had worked in a bike shop and was never particularly impressed by the workmanship on even the most expensive bikes. His passion for building bikes came from an overwhelming urge to create something with his own hands and he knew he could create something much better than the mass-produced models that he had seen in his youth.

With every bike he builds, Keith tries to incorporate some type of unique design element and aims to never build the same bike twice. He always looks for ways to personalize a bike for a customer and is very focused on detail, not only for aesthetics but also for functionality. All of Keith Anderson's bikes are built exclusively with steel because he believes that it has a history unmatched by any other material used by man. It has all the properties necessary to make the perfect bicycle—strength, durability, resilience, is easily repairable, readily available, relatively cheap, and compared to titanium, aluminum, and carbon fiber, less toxic to produce. "Once put into its final form, steel has a ride that cannot be duplicated."

As someone who has a highly developed artistic flair, Keith feels blessed that he's always had a diverse skill set that has led to him being a bike builder and painter. He is not only highly regarded as a frame builder but also as a master painter of bicycle frames, and much of his time is spent doing paintwork for other builders. Although he loves every aspect of the bike-building process, Keith says, "The transformation that takes place during the painting process is like a butterfly emerging from its chrysalis. It has metamorphosed from something dark and monochromatic into something rich and colorful."

Like any business, there are other aspects to be taken care of and Keith's assistant Corey helps him to keep focused on production. Corey takes care of the digital artwork creation, website development, answering phones, shipping, and whatever else it takes to run a contemporary bike-building business. Music is also a constant in Keith and Corey's working day and is played through a CD changer, a decent-sized amp, and four booming speakers. The workspace also includes a couple of guitars and a drum set ready for those times when inspiration strikes and also for Keith and Corey to have a jam session at the end of the day. They always have fun at work, which Keith believes is an important ingredient in maintaining a good working environment. Apart from the Keith Anderson head badge, affectionately know as "Howdy Sprocket," Keith's favorite feature on a bike is the rider: "Without the rider it's just a piece of functional art … bicycles are just like guitars, they are tools to be used no matter how beautiful."

"Without the rider it's just a piece of functional art …
bicycles are just like guitars, they are tools to be used no
matter how beautiful."

Keith Anderson logo in 24k gold leaf

"The transformation that takes place during the painting process is like a butterfly emerging from its chrysalis. It has metamorphosed from something dark and monochromatic into something rich and colorful."

Etched sterling-silver head badge

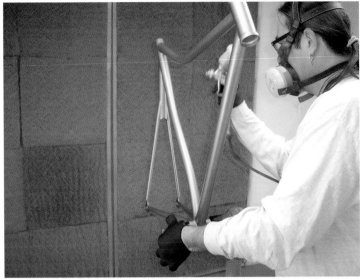

Applying multiple coats of blue candy to a pursuit frame

Seat cluster showing seat stay top before cap

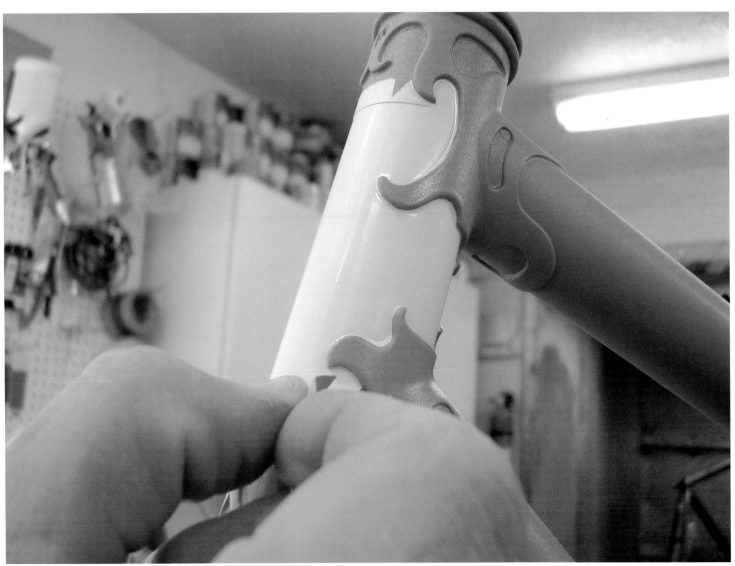

Unmasking the head tube on a Rivendell

Kirk Frameworks

Bozeman, Montana USA

David Kirk was too young to have one of the racing cars his father built so he had the next best thing, a British Racing Green bicycle with his name emblazoned across the chain guard in chrome lettering. David's father was a racing car mechanic and when it came time for David to get his first bicycle he made one from parts he collected and refurbished, with some new parts thrown into the mix. David had a unique, custom-made bike that opened up his world and allowed him to explore things on his own for the first time. His father instilled in him from day one the concept that bicycles were something one made and not something one bought.

Many years have passed between that first bicycle and David becoming a frame builder, but he always knew it would happen, as if he was born to it. Like the cars his father worked on, David's bikes are designed to perform. He likes to think of them as simple and elegant with a look that draws you in for a closer inspection, as opposed to something that shouts at you. As David explains: "They are sparse and to the point. My favorite car is a Lotus Seven and I would be pleased to have my bikes compared to one." All of David's bikes are built from steel and are either lugged and silver brazed or fillet brazed with brass. He loves the way steel rides and the feeling it gives on the road, and having worked with many other materials he prefers it because nothing compares to the way it feels in his hands and the sound it makes when working with it.

As a lone builder, David is involved in all aspects of building, right down to shipping the bikes to their new owners. All Kirk bikes are produced in his garage at home, which has everything he needs plus the added bonus of incredible mountain views. When David constructs his frames he does it in two phases. First the front triangle is built and machined straight and clean, then the rear triangle is added to the front. He believes that working on the front triangle before the rear is added is much easier and more efficient. Adding the rear triangle to the front allows a view of the entire bike in his mind's eye and enables him to visualize it under the rider on the road, doing what it's meant to do. "Adding the rear is my favorite part because it turns the work from a bunch of tubes to a frame. Even after all these years and thousands of frames I still get excited every time I add the rear triangle."

David's favorite part on a bike is the seat cluster because there are four tubes coming together plus the seat post clamp. He likes putting a lot of detail into this area to make it a visual focal point. As a homage to his father, David's DK logo was inspired by the way his father used to mark his own specialized automotive tools with a JK where the back of the J and K were shared. He has also continued his father's love of racing cars by fabricating his own parts and entering autocross events. At the end of the day, David takes time out to look over his work, then watches the orange light of the sunset shining on the Bridger Mountains right in front of his home.

"Adding the rear is my favorite part because it turns the work from a bunch of tubes to a frame. Even after all these years and thousands of frames I still get excited every time I add the rear triangle."

JK Special road race bike

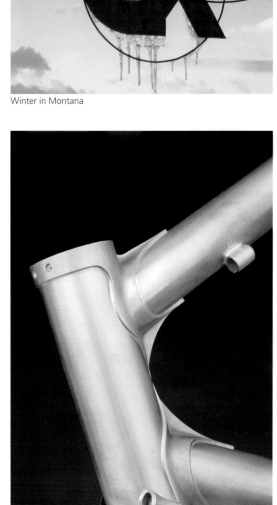

Winter in Montana

Self portrait in shop

Webbed lugs in the raw

Playing with fire

Unpainted fillet brazed bottom bracket

"My favorite car is a Lotus Seven and I would be pleased to have my bikes compared to one."

Still looks wet

The downhill ride was a thrill …

"I finally got to take my bike up and down a twisting mountain road today and, I can tell you without a doubt, this is the best handling bike I have ever had the privilege of riding. This bike climbed effortlessly without a lot of input on my part. I didn't have to fight to keep my line, though it was responsive when asked to be. The downhill ride was a thrill. I didn't think it was possible, but the bike felt so stable and nimble at the same time. From the very first turn it was silky smooth, though not in the least sluggish. I could drive into a curve and, if need be, change my line at the last minute to maneuver around rocks or sand without any hesitation or protest from the bike. It entered and exited the turns exactly as I wanted and made me wish the ride was longer, something that I haven't experienced in a long time. Dave, I don't know how you did it, but you have the magic touch; I wouldn't change a thing."

Anonymous

Orange and blue

Karin Kirk high in the Bridger Mountains

Ice blue Terraplane

Crisp lug lines and bespoke brass cable adjusters

Kish Fabrication

San Luis Obispo, California USA

Performing major surgery on broken bicycles to get to the next destination played a significant part in Jim Kish becoming a bicycle frame builder. After several years of living out of panniers as a professional bicycle tour leader, Jim needed a new path to follow. One of his favorite parts of touring was the challenge of fixing bikes, so it seemed to be an easy choice to embark on creating his own bike-building business in 1992.

Kish bikes are designed to be as efficient and as simple as possible; nothing is there that doesn't belong. Even the head badge on his bikes is a small, simple K with no interesting story behind it other than it's K for Kish. Jim builds his bikes from titanium and steel, but prefers titanium because he feels it exhibits the perfect combination: it's strong, lightweight, corrosion resistant, and provides a smooth ride. In its unpainted state, titanium also has an elegant, yet utilitarian look.

Jim's frame-building philosophy is also reflected in his workspace, which is relatively compact, stocked with very fine tools and fixtures, and kept very clean. If you were to wander into Jim's workspace today, you may hear some psychedelic rock, ambient, bluegrass, or metal music wafting from the stereo system, as music provides a constant backdrop to his working day. His dog is also there to keep him company as she sleeps away the day on her bed. Jim's workshop space, tools, and equipment also come in handy for both family and friends when something needs fixing or to build car parts, furniture, or any other widget that may be needed.

The problem solving process of the fitting and frame design are Jim's favorite part of bike building. When taking a customer's body and current bike measurements, he also weighs up their athletic experience and riding style. Jim believes that while most people could fit comfortably on a stock bicycle, everyone can benefit in some way by owning a custom-built bike. It may simply be a detail in the fit, the tubing selection to complement riding style, or the fittings to match individual needs or aesthetic preference that make it all worthwhile. Jim has particularly enjoyed working with some of his customers who have been architects, photographers, and musicians because they have all shared a similar sense of a bicycle's purpose and a "less is more" aesthetic.

Jim is kept very busy these days building bikes for other people to ride. He no longer has the time to go on long bike tours, but he does use his bike to run errands and tries to get out on a long mountain or road ride at least once a week. For Jim: "The ultimate feature of a bike is its intangible capability to motivate one to ride more and get healthier."

Town bike with rack

TI road bike with back end

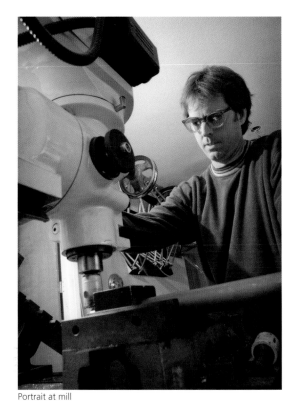

Portrait at mill

Welding

"The ultimate feature of a bike is its intangible capability to motivate one to ride more and get healthier."

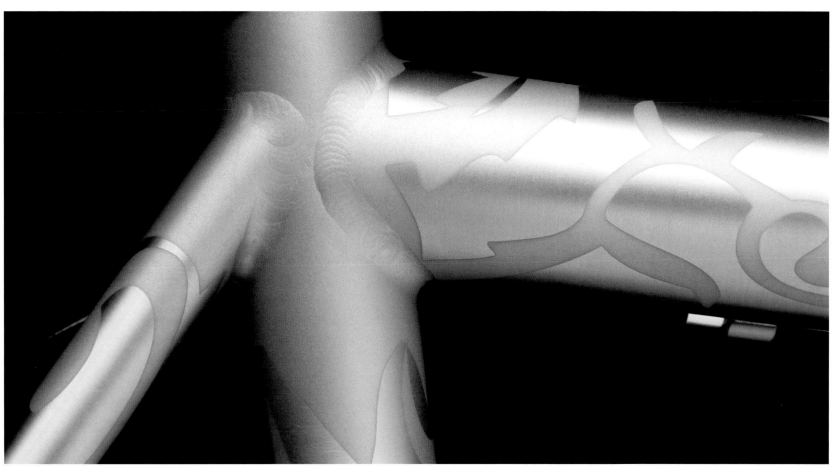

Etched TI road bike

Painted TI 29er

Mountain bike bottom bracket

Jim's process is clear and enlightening ...

"After researching many titanium frame builders, I finally decided to meet with Jim Kish first and I never contacted any other builder. From the outset, his courtesy, experience, attention to detail, enthusiasm, and professionalism were clearly evident. I immediately ordered a custom titanium and I have been completely satisfied ever since. Jim's process is clear and enlightening, the fit is perfect, the craftsmanship is excellent, the finish is gorgeous, and the ride is superb."

Tomaso Bradshaw, Venice California

650 B MTN bike

Llewellyn Custom Bicycles

Everton Hills, Queensland Australia

From an early age, the young Darrell McCulloch played intensely with his Lego. This creative focus was a precursor to building model railways and Airfix plane kits as he grew older. At school he was naturally drawn to art, woodwork, metalwork, and technical drawing, and at home he was always tinkering with bikes. Fitness has been an important part of Darrell's life from a young age; his family didn't own a car so bikes were a natural choice of transport. Two Bicycling magazine articles describing custom bicycle frame building and a story about a team mechanic further sparked Darrell's passion for bikes and cycling. At this point in time he was a keen athletics competitor, but decided to switch from athletics to cycle racing as his interests in all things bicycle grew stronger.

After leaving school, Darrell got a job with one of the few frame builders in Queensland and worked with him for six and a half years and later in other bike shops. Darrell had a vision of where he wanted to be and established Llewellyn Custom Bicycles toward the end of 1988 as a part time affair. During this period he was also racing bikes in France, working with cycling teams as a mechanic, and coming home

for the summer. He counts himself very fortunate that he had the experience of traveling to 21 different countries with the Australian Institute of Sport as their road cycling mechanic and an equipment supplier for the men's and women's road teams. By 2001, Darrell chose to fully devote his energies to Llewellyn Custom Bicycles because he knew that building bespoke bicycles was how he wanted to express himself.

Over the years, Darrell has developed and pursued his own style and techniques for creating beautifully crafted lugged-steel bicycles. His grandfather's words, "Don't rest till your best is better," are always an inspiration to Darrell and each week he sets out to better what he did the week before at the workbench. "Many details and techniques would make not one difference to the client's perception of their Llewellyn cycle, but are done for my satisfaction. For me to know that a particular detail or step is inserted sates my pursuit of purity in the frame construction process."

Darrell uses high-quality butted-steel tubing and lugged construction for its superb ride qualities and

proven durability. This method offers endless possibilities and flexibility for his expression of design and aesthetics, including intricate detailing when desired. Many parts and features on a Llewellyn bike are made from stainless steel because he feels this material also has merit. Aesthetics are important to Darrell, but durability and function will never be sacrificed. "My desire is to create a bicycle for my client that gives them many years of enjoyable riding, so with each passing year the bicycle gives them more value. Thus they come to cherish their Llewellyn."

Darrell works alone at the bench, manipulating the tubes and lugs, wielding the brazing torch, and guiding the files with his hands. His painter Joe Cosgrove gives each Llewellyn bike its beautiful paint finish, allowing Darrell to be intensely absorbed with the design and form of the metalwork. In keeping with his lifetime of fitness, Darrell gets out to ride most days for two or three hours in the surrounding hills and mountains, with a longer ride with his mates on Sundays. Bikes have given Darrell many great travels and friends from around the world and he is grateful that his passion is constantly fed from the enjoyment he gets from clients using his bicycles.

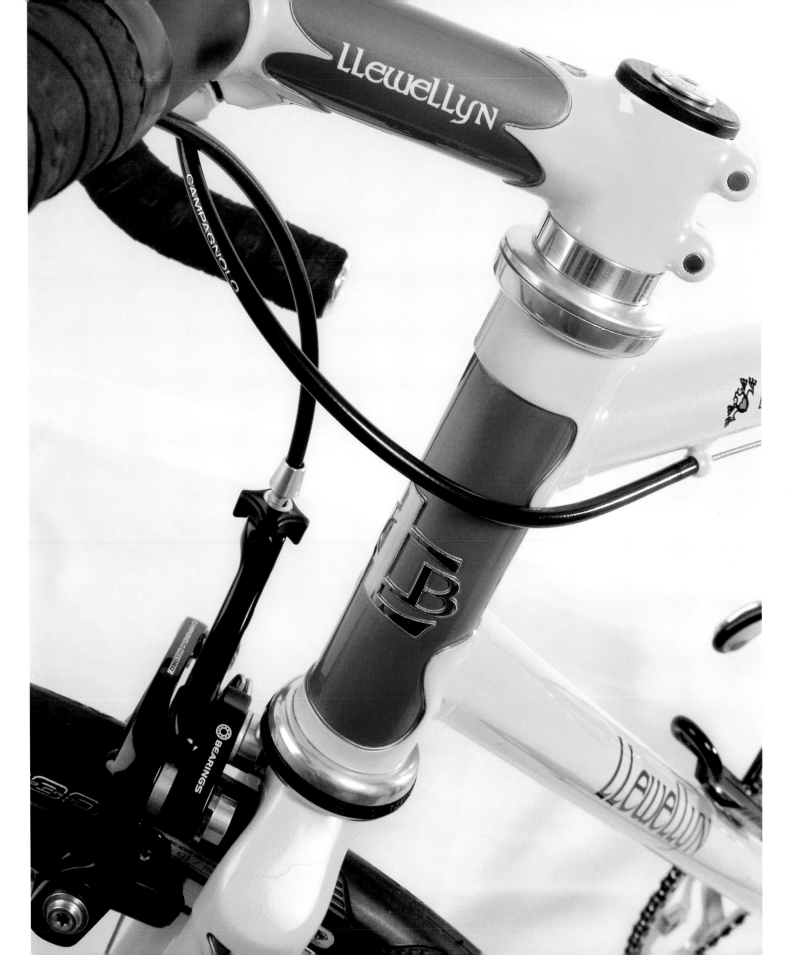

Finish work on a lugged stem

Nine hours were spent on this custom handmade lug

Stainless steel details

At the alignment table

"Many details and techniques would make not one difference to the client's perception of their Llewellyn cycle, but are done for my satisfaction. For me to know that a particular detail or step is inserted is to sate my pursuit of purity in the frame construction process."

It feels like nothing I've ever ridden ...

"By way of touring bike—completely assured, responsive, poised, and gorgeous to look at. A friend described it as an interesting mix of retro looks (the frame geometry, quill, cantilever brakes, and color scheme) coupled with modern components. I think he's right. At first glance it looks like a well-preserved 35-year-old bike, but on closer examination you realize that all the components are current. It leans beautifully into corners, the cantilever brakes pull it up much better than side-pulls ever could, it absorbs road shocks exceptionally well and exceptionally quietly, and it doesn't complain about anything I throw at it but seems to keep saying "bring it on—is that all you've got?"

Christopher L.

Details cut into stainless steel dropouts

Hand-cut and polished stainless lugs

Hand-cut stainless details

No chrome! Llewellyn with stainless lugs.

Luna Cycles

Santa Fe, New Mexico USA

Margo Conover is a bicycle frame builder who markets her products to women cyclists. Her company, Luna Cycles, has been specializing in building bikes for women since 1995, and Margo is one of only a few women in the male-dominated profession of bike building.

Margo's life and work are located in beautiful Santa Fe, New Mexico. Seven years of bike racing and time spent as a bike mechanic have given her plenty of experience in understanding how a bike functions and performs, and Margo naturally found herself gravitating towards working as a bike-frame builder, a profession she had always admired. Having often ridden poorly fitted bikes, the inspiration for wanting to build bikes better-suited to women came from a desire to figure out why obtaining a good fit was so difficult for her to achieve.

According to Margo, there are numerous female-specific aspects that can affect the riding position, particularly a woman's anatomy on the seat. Often women are uncomfortable on their saddle and their position on the bike can exacerbate that discomfort. Margo believes that her customers have an inherent trust in her ability to address issues of discomfort because she has been both cycling and constructing bikes for a long time, and of course because she has experienced similar issues herself.

As the majority of her customers live outside her local area, many of the details that she requires to build a frame are initially gained from a questionnaire, which forms the basis for much discussion over the internet or via telephone. Gaining critical body measurements and information, such as the likes and dislikes of their current bike in terms of fit and performance, are vital pieces of information that help Margo understand each woman's needs before she begins designing a bike frame. At first, Margo was skeptical of anything other than a dynamic face-to-face fit, but over the years her fitting methods have consistently worked.

The style of bikes that Margo Conover builds reflects where she lives and rides, and her standard customer is someone in their 40s who is a serious recreational rider. Although these days she doesn't get out on her own bike as much as she would like, when she does, Margo is constantly reminded of how much she enjoys riding. The Luna Cycles head badge, designed by a jeweler friend of Margo's, depicts a moon over a mountain, much like the view outside the window of her home when she lived in Colorado. Since taking on the quest to find the perfect fit, Margo now rides in a position that is comfortable and efficient. She believes that: "The key to efficiency is feeling comfortable on your bike, and then you can power on."

Single-speed resting against an adobe wall in Santa Fe, New Mexico

Deep purple cyclocross frame

Custom 26-inch cyclocross fork

This baby just wants to fly …

"I've got over 1,000 miles on my Luna now. I call it my 'pocket-rocket'—this baby just wants to fly! The ride is incredible on this machine. I'm passing people on flats, downhill coasts, and to my joy I've actually passed people on hill climbs! The handling is super tight and I'm finding I can take corners and curves with a greater proficiency then ever before. The ladies I ride with have drooled over my bike and said 'It's the prettiest baby they've ever seen.' All the guys at Montlake Bicycle Shop in Seattle, who did my pedal fit and checkout, stood around and admired the bike."

Deb Lazetti Bellevue, Washington

Road frame and fork

Custom cyclocross bike in the old mining town of Eldora, Colorado

"The key to efficiency is feeling comfortable on your bike, and then you can power on."

Front-end detail on Campy-equipped road Luna

This bicycle was picked up in person by a sweet man from Manitoba, Canada. He ordered it for his wife who is undergoing chemotherapy for breast cancer at 34 years old. They are both avid cyclists, and this gift was to inspire healing during those periods between treatments when she had enough energy to go outside and ride. Hubs and headset are Chris King special edition pink, with proceeds benefiting breast cancer research.

Lynskey

Chattanooga, Tennessee USA

Lynskey is very a much a family-operated company with a burning desire to produce high-quality, custom-made performance bikes that are also functional pieces of art. Mark Lynskey and his siblings grew up around the tools and machinery of their father's Chattanooga machine shop, which was established in the 1960s when Chattanooga was one of the largest industrial centers in the United States. Mark Lynskey is a mechanical engineer by profession and specialized in exotic metals fabrication. It was through one of Mark's younger brothers that the family turned their experience and expertise of metal fabrication into making bikes.

David Lynskey took up cycling when he had to give up running because of a knee injury. When it came to getting a bike for himself, it was a natural progression to look no further than his family's machining business. By the late 1980s, after David had made other bikes for friends, it was clear to the family that David's bike building was a path that they wanted to pursue and they were interested in producing their own brand of bicycles. The idea proved to be highly successful, and by the mid 1990s it was all that the business was producing.

Over that time, they built a reputation as a world leader in high-performance titanium bikes and was eventually acquired by another company.

After a period of time, the Lynskey family decided that they wanted to do something together, and through their mother Ruby's encouragement it was decided that they would again start building bicycles because of their love of working with metal and their desire to be involved with an active sport. The family enjoys working with elite athletes through to recreational riders and loves the challenge of building bikes that are not just individually tailored, but also high performance and suited to owners' particular needs. The real spirit and goal of what they are constantly trying to achieve is: "To have a bike that does exactly what you want it to do, fits you exactly the way you want it to fit, and looks exactly as your heart desires."

The five members of the Lynskey family all have their designated roles in the business and have complementary skills for producing their range of custom bikes. Mark's primary roles are bike design, sales, and marketing; the next eldest brother, David, is also involved with the bike designs and oversees the running of the workshop as well as designing tools and equipment. The second youngest brother is Chris, who does all of the engineering drawings, his wife Toni is the welder, and the youngest brother Tim runs the finishing department and final inspection. Finally, Ruby and her daughter Theresa play active roles in the business on a daily basis by running the accounts department. Although Mark Lynskey's father passed away a number of years ago, he is still very much a part of the Lynskey brand with his signature appearing on the head badge. Also featured on the badge is a shamrock, as Lynskey is an Irish name, and a tethered hunting hawk from the Thompson family crest, which refers to their mother's maiden name and British heritage.

An R420 was donated to Sgt. Lee Robbs of the Chattanooga Police Department for the Police Unity Tour

This complete custom cruiser-style 29er is a wolf in sheep's clothing

Helix Technology tubeset after mitering and before welding, shown on a full-size CAD drawing

A custom Level 4 frameset built for a customer in Atlanta, Georgia

Detail of a belt-drive road bike's rear stay; this breakaway section allows for the belt to fit inside the rear triangle

BURN 24 Hour
120
55ninePerformance.com

The end of a long day's racing—Lynskey Pro29 after many, many miles and 24 hours of racing

"To have a bike that does exactly what you want it to do, fits you exactly the way you want it to fit, and looks exactly as your heart desires."

This R420 was built for Sugar Cycles in Texas

This complete mountain bike is a custom Level 3 with 650B wheels built for Richard Cunningham of Mountain Bike Action

The Lynskey tricycle

Marschall Framework

Moehnesee, Germany

Uwe Marschall's passion for bikes was ignited at the age of 13, when he visited a bike workshop. As he grew older, he began competing in bike races with much success. As a lone frame builder, Uwe has been constructing tailor-made road racing, touring, and mountain bikes since 1991, and also makes child-sized bikes and tandems. The inspiration for his designs is taken from the classic Italian designs, noted for their clean lines and aesthetic appeal.

His choice of frame building material is steel and stainless steel, which he prefers for their strength and versatility. The frames can be finished in a shining wet lacquer or a natural non-lacquered look that can be brushed finished or highly polished, using high-grade steel. For those customers who wish to add

color to their frame, there are a number of specialized paintwork designs and colors from which to choose. Uwe also likes to build with steel because, from an environmental point of view, he believes it is far more eco-friendly than other materials, due to less energy consumption in the extraction process.

Building a bike that fits a customer exactly is paramount to Uwe, and he therefore conducts an exhaustive measuring process plus detailed discussion on personal preferences and the purpose for which the bike will be ridden. All of these elements are taken into consideration before Uwe enters the data into a specialized computer program that he uses to

calculate and determine to correct geometry for the bike frame. One of the most important features to be placed on his bikes is the Marschall Framework star. The head badge is the final piece to be placed on any individual bike before it is handed over to the customer. For Uwe, it marks the end of his building process and the beginning of a wonderful riding experience for the new owner.

Moots

Steamboat Springs, Colorado USA

Moots is located high in the mountains in a little ski resort town called Steamboat Springs. It's a very remote area and sits at about 7,000 feet of elevation on the west side of the Rockies. The 20 full-time employees work in a modern, clean facility and are very much a part of the town community; they help the locals maintain a piece of forested property that has world-class trails and is located just above the town. During the summer months, mountain bike riders have access to miles of pristine, tall-wooded areas in which to enjoy the fresh mountain air while riding their bikes along sun-filtered trails.

As a company, Moots aims to be environmentally responsible by keeping cars out of their parking lot as much as possible. They encourage their employees to ride to work and have a company commute policy where employees earn credits towards bike parts. It's all part of a broader Moots philosophy to build beautiful bikes with a ride quality that will find you choosing to ride to work or run errands on your bike rather than taking the car. Their regard for the environment also permeates through the workplace, where they recycle everything they use, including all metals and cardboard, instead of sending it to landfill.

The Moots staff come from a wide variety of backgrounds and whether they have worked in bike shops, studied bike building at frame school, toured the world on a bike, or raced professionally, they all have something in common—a passion for bikes and cycling.

When Moots started building bikes in 1981, they built nothing but steel custom road bikes, which then evolved into their first steel mountain bike. In 1990, Moots switched to making bikes from titanium and have since been thoroughly dedicated to building all their bikes from this material. As a metal, titanium not only suits the Moots philosophy of building a product that is long lasting, but it also works well with their bike designs.

It's important to Moots that their customers have an enjoyable experience right from the beginning because most often they have saved and saved for the bike of their dreams, and when people are spending that sort of money it's important that everything is done correctly. The Moots custom-fitting process is facilitated through their vast, worldwide dealer network and they only seek out high-quality dealers who are experienced and efficient in the fitting process.

As a testament to handmade custom bicycles being bikes for a lifetime, customers will often send bikes that they've owned for many years back to the Moots factory to be reblasted and decaled. The holistic approach that Moots has developed over the years towards its employees, their community, the environment, their bike building, and ultimately their customers, is a model to be proud of. The Moots philosophy is reflected in the clean lines of their bike designs and the idea that a well-made bike crafted by highly skilled people can become an heirloom that is passed on through families for many years to come.

Vamoots … titanium smoothness for the road

The classic YBB ("why be beat") provides pivotless suspension technology

The Moots workshop

Julie leading the lunchtime loop

Mootour frame with signature headbadge

Jon blazing on his Psychlo X

Mike Curiak's custom Snoots, Alaska Range Alaska

Afternoon pedal through the Aspens

Thanks Moots ...

"I went to Moots with a pretty firm idea of what I wanted in a custom bike. It turns out there is far more to a custom bike than I was aware of, and some of my ideas were simply not going to work. Moots patiently educated me on what my options were at each step in the process, and the result is, well ... you can see for yourself that there's no other bike on the planet even remotely like mine. Thanks Moots."

Mike Curiak, Ultra Marathon Bike Record Holder

Naked Bicycles and Design

Quadra Island, BC Canada

Naked Bicycles and Design, run by Sam Whittingham and his wife Andrea, is located on Quadra Island, four hours north of Victoria, British Columbia, and is accessible by a small ferry from Vancouver Island. The workshop's remote location means that many Naked bikes are built by long-distance correspondence with the client, so detailed conversations by the telephone or the Internet are extremely important to the fitting and design process. However, when Sam meets customers face-to-face he relishes the opportunity to perform a personalized fitting. As part of this fitting process, Sam likes to head out for a ride with his customers so that he can fully analyze each client's riding style, skill level, and ride preferences. In order for Sam to custom build the right bike, it is vital that he understands both the personality and cycling needs of his customers.

Sam's driving passion to build bikes was nurtured by doing a lot of bike touring with his dad. He has also raced both mountain and track bikes and was on the Canadian National Track Team for a number of years; remarkably, one of his claims to fame is his inclusion in the Guinness Book of Records for a speed bike record. Before he embarked on setting up his own bike-building business, Sam worked for many years as a bike fitter and spent a lot of time measuring customers and working off their current bikes. This experience helped shape his bike-building philosophy: "Fitting the man to the machine, that's my thing. Making them one with the bike, which you can only do with custom."

The name Naked reflects one of Sam's core attitudes: "My desire is to build bikes unadulterated by hype and the latest fads." For Sam, it is crucial that his custom bikes not only fit each customer perfectly, but are also reliable and built to last: "I know I can build a steel bike that in 20 years is not going to crack." Although Sam is mostly called upon to build basic, everyday TIG-welded bikes, he is able to indulge in more intricate design features when a customer requests a lugged bike. With a background in theatrical costume and set design, Sam's creative skills really come to the fore when he wants to build a special bike. For the 2007 North American Handmade Bike Show, Sam combined all of his bike-building skills and creative flair to build an exceptional show bike. Features such as wooden wheel rims, the extensive use of chrome, and angled sculptured handlebars with wooden grips caught the eye of a Tour de France winner, who subsequently acquired the award-winning bike for his collection.

Sam Whittingham's passion for building bikes is often reflected back to him from his equally passionate customers. He has one such client who regularly keeps Sam updated with the life and times of his bike by sending him pictures of his cycling adventures. Whether Sam's breaking speed records or designing eye catching show bikes, you can be sure that Naked is about form, function, and line.

Sam leads the pack

"Fitting the man to the machine, that's my thing. Making them one with the bike, which you can only do with custom."

The bike rocks …

"It climbs fast, isn't twitchy on the downhill, and it rails turns.
The bike rocks, you did a great job!"

Mike Morgan, California

All paint is done in the Naked workshop

Naked fabricates many of its own parts

All Naked bikes are built with love and logic

Custom spoke shave handlebars

"My desire is to build bikes unadulterated by hype and the latest fads."

Baba Ganoush—NAHBS 2008 Best in Show-winning bike

Naked detailing, including e-centric dropouts

Pegoretti

Trento, Italy

Dario Pegoretti's journey into bike building began out of necessity—his father-in-law required some help in his workshop and Dario needed some cash. Although he admits the passion grew slowly, once it was ignited he developed a true hunger to start building his own frames. After learning his craft from Gino Milani in the great Italian frame-building tradition, Dario was keen to apply his own ideas to frame building.

Over the years, Dario built up a reputation in the professional riding scene, and found himself building frames for elite riders and teams in Europe because of the particular ride characteristics of his bikes. Dario also raced as a young man, but doesn't get out to ride as much as he would like these days because he is so busy creating bikes for customers. Dario's workshop is located in Caldonazzo, a beautiful resort town in the Dolomites, just a few minutes from his home, near Trento.

Dario builds a range of bikes from steel and aluminum, but has a preference for steel because it allows for the most control in the building process and provides the best ride qualities. Pegoretti bikes also have a reputation for their unique paint schemes, optional designs, colors, and finishes, which transform the bike into a rolling piece of art. When somebody owns a custom Pegoretti bike, they not only have a bike that suits their body and riding requirements, but will also be riding on top of more than 25 years of experience from a master builder who has put his own stamp on bike design and built bikes for some of the top riders in the world.

It is very important to Dario for people to understand that his bikes are handmade, and this is evident in his head badge. The Pegoretti head badge, which is fixed to the frame with machine screws, is made of steel with a stylized "P" and a hand to signify that the frame is *fatti con le mani*, "made with hands." Assisted by Pietro and Daniel in his workshop, many a Pegoretti bike has been born to the sounds of blues and jazz floating through the workshop from the horn speakers and valve amplifier.

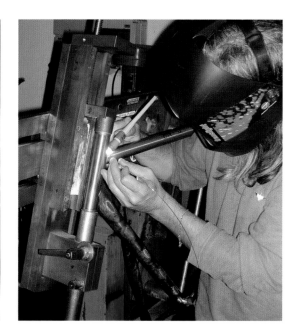

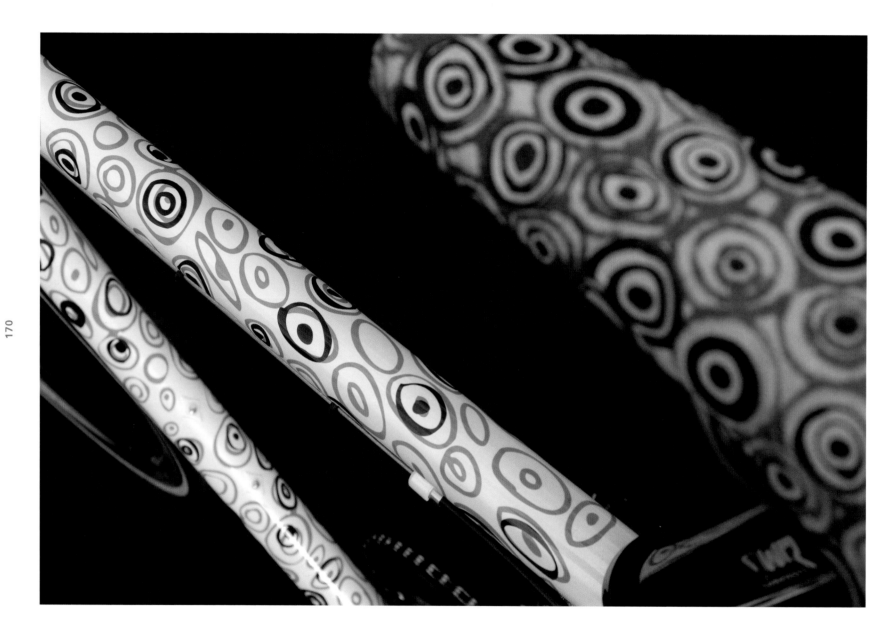

Richard Sachs Cycles

Chester, Connecticut USA

A self-confessed rebel, Richard Sachs describes his passion and addiction to bikes and racing as continually evolving and believes that he came to bike building serendipitously. At the age of 16, he was smitten with his 10-speed bike and eventually started subscribing to biking magazines and learning about bike racing. What he does as a bike builder is inseparable from the sport of racing, something that became embedded in his psyche back in the 1960s: "The needle kind of got in my arm once I learned the connection between bicycles and the sport of bike racing." On completing high school he couldn't get into college in September and had to wait until April. With time to kill, he wrote several bike builders in England hoping that he'd be able to travel and learn how to make bikes. Fortunately, one person offered him such an opportunity, and he headed off to England for a year and worked as an apprentice at Witcomb Cycles.

Richard is also a confirmed loner and over the years has never felt the need to take on an apprentice himself for various reasons. He and many of his contemporaries learned their craft hands-on in the bicycle production arenas and he believes that without doing tasks repetitively and without seeing things done time after time, hour after hour, you can't possibly glean enough from a frame builder to become a frame builder. As a master frame builder himself with more than 35 years' experience, Richard believes that the learning never ends and that you never fully understand what you're doing. As he says, "You can believe you've mastered it or attained it, but before you know it something will happen and after all those years you've been doing it a certain way, you just realize that you can do it better or more efficiently."

Richard not only tries to perfect his own skills on a daily basis, but is also passionate about passing on his knowledge and experience to others in his own way. As a prolific blogger, he spends a lot of time on message boards answering questions and providing links to his Flickr pages. There is also the Richard Sachs cyclocross team, in which Richard regularly competes with just as much conviction as in his younger days. He has been told on numerous occasions that: "He's got it licked." He works for himself, he likes what he does, he's in demand, and he describes the town where he lives as like heaven on earth.

Richard and his wife live in a two-story building with a couple of courtyards. His workshop is located on the ground floor and opens onto a European style, redbrick courtyard filled with plants and flowers. His dog sleeps in a chair while he's building and the cat comes and goes as it pleases. Richard is totally focused when building and likes to work in silence, as to him any sound is a distraction that takes him away from being at one with the art of frame building. The type of customer who wants a Richard Sachs lugged-steel racing bike comes to him with an understanding of his emotions, his thoughts, and his racing team, and after being in the business for a long time, Richard feels blessed that the kind of orders he gets suits the type of bikes that he wants to make.

"The needle kind of got in my arm once I learned the connection between bicycles and the sport of bike racing."

"You can believe you've mastered it or attained it, but before you know it something will happen and after all those years you've been doing it a certain way, you just realised you can do it better or more efficiently."

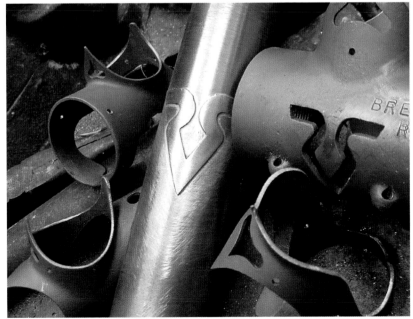

Roark Custom Titanium Bicycles

Brownsburg, Indiana USA

Roark is an aerospace company that has been producing jet engine parts for more than 55 years. Within the same facility, a group of three employees also makes beautifully crafted titanium bikes. This connection between bicycles and flying has a famous precedent—the Wright brothers drew inspiration for developing their flying machines from bicycles. According to Jim Zoellner, one of the bike-building team, Roark, as opposed to the Wright brothers, took their inspiration from the aerospace industry and applied their specific knowledge of aviation to the design and production of titanium bicycles.

Roark builds a range of custom bikes that are designed to perfectly suit each individual rider. There are two local fitters in Indianapolis and authorized fitters all over the world; these technicians fit each customer on an adjustable-fit bike and spend two to three hours with them making the necessary adjustments and discussing the fit and measurements. Once the session is complete, this information is sent to the bike-building team at Roark and the frame is designed accordingly. With access to the best materials and equipment, highly skilled industrial designers, and metal workers, Roark is able to build high-quality

custom bikes for people with a great passion for cycling, whether they are casual riders or hardcore racers. Over the past ten years, the company has also sponsored one of the top amateur cycling teams in the United States, the Texas Roadhouse Cycling Team. The team has been very successful and has won approximately 20 national championships riding Roark racing bikes.

The bike-building team at Roark are not only adept at building a wide range of bikes, but when a special bike order is called for they are limited only by their imagination in utilizing the high-tech equipment and incorporating aerospace materials into the design. Jim Zoellner wanted to make a special bike for his young daughter and came up with the idea of laser-cut butterfly wheel spokes, which is only one of the many distinguishing artistic features on this bicycle. The head badge and butterflies dotted all over the bike's frame were made from a stainless-steel mesh designed for use on a nuclear submarine. With its curved tubing frame design, custom chain guard,

and personally engraved seat, it is the type of bike that can go on to become a family heirloom: "The bike is a beautiful thing. You think back to some of your best childhood memories and many of them do contain bicycles."

Roark track bike—2007 NAHBS Best Titanium Bike

"The bike is a beautiful thing. You think back to some of your best childhood memories and many of them do contain bicycles."

Titanium chain guard

SRAM I-Motion 9-speed hub resides inside custom billet 16-inch wheel

Roark show bike for 2008 NAHBS

Robin Mather

Upper Wraxall, United Kingdom

A few miles north of Bath, in the village of Upper Wraxall, Robin Mather has been building lugged and fillet-brazed steel frames for the past 15 years. The passion that drives him more than anything else is the creative process in the workshop and being able to lose himself in imagining, designing, and finally realizing a small detail. Robin has always been interested in how things are constructed and grew up in a woodworking environment where tools, equipment, and workshop space were always available. He believes that there is something intrinsically wonderful about cycling and is not driven by the belief that there is only one-way to build a bicycle.

Robin started building frames with steel because of its relative affordability and because he feels that as a material it offers plenty of opportunities and challenges. Although he is also interested in the possibilities of other materials, he is content to leave it for other bike-builders to explore. Each frame he makes is individually considered and is the end result of the customer's needs and preferences. Robin Mather likes to innovate, but is well aware of the 100 years of evolution that the bicycle has undergone.

He derives satisfaction from executing conventional design well and ensuring that every detail of the bike is perfectly finished. In his own way, he also likes to advocate the use of bikes for transport and particularly enjoys making functional, versatile bikes.

Robin's approach to bike fitting is flexible as he builds a wide range of bike types, from expedition tourers to fast randonneur and single-speed 29ers, and doesn't believe that there is one fit system that can cope with every situation. He places great emphasis on a customer's existing bike and their subjective experience as well as finding out the intended function, level of fitness, flexibility, and aspirations of each customer. Where possible, he also likes to go for a short ride with his clients to observe their riding style. A labyrinth of small, relatively traffic-free country roads surround Robin's workshop space. It's not only perfect to take customers for a ride, but Robin likes to get out as often as he can for a brisk 30-mile morning ride. Occasionally, he will head off-road and he loves to tour in France and has also taken trips in Italy, Ethiopia, Iceland, and Norway.

Like many frame builders, Robin Mather's business has grown organically out of a hobby, by first building bikes for himself, then for friends who have become customers. He is now fortunate that many of his customers have become friends.

Custom-made stainless-steel rack on a fixed-gear randonneur bike

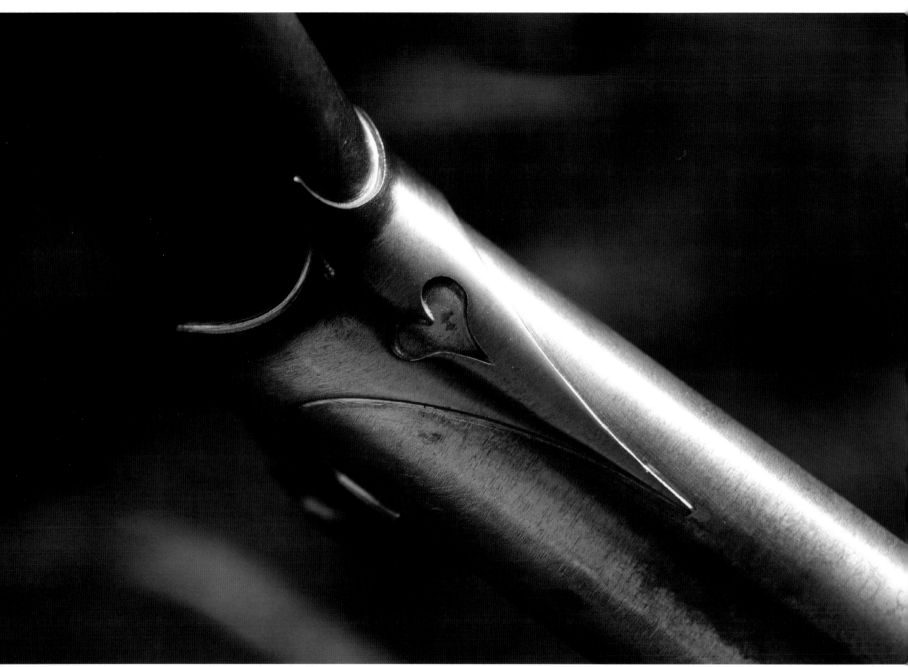

Reynolds 725 tubes silver-brazed into a modified Pacenti bottom head lug

Adding brass fillet to bottom bracket of a single-speed mountain bike

Fillet-brazed stem with captive wedge-style binder, lamp mount, and integrated top cap

Hand-cut stainless-steel head badge

Custom-made stainless-steel rack on a fixed-gear randonneur bike

Fixed-gear randonneur bike in Reynolds 725 with Sachs Newvex lugs and custom-made stem and rack

Chrome-plated, fillet-brazed stem with captive wedge-style binder, lamp mount, and integrated top cap

Fixed-gear randonneur bike in Reynolds 725, with Sachs Newvex lugs and custom-made stem and rack

Single-speed mountain bike in Reynolds 853, with Columbus seat stays and fork blades

Signal Cycles

Portland, Oregon USA

Signal Cycles entered the custom bike-building industry when two art school graduates, Nate Meschke and Matt Cardinal, launched their company in February 2008. Nate and Matt were drawn to the art of bike building because it combines their love of cycling with the ability to work with their hands, and also serves as an outlet for creative expression that enables them to build objects that are both beautiful and practical.

When Matt was seven years old he had a much-loved BMX bike that he decided to pull apart for a clean and to see how it worked. Although it seemed a good idea at the time, when it came to putting the bike back together he had no idea how to reassemble the pile of parts that sat before him. Over the next 15 years, Matt honed his skills as a bike mechanic and artist, and developed a broader appreciation for the bicycle. Nate also worked in a bike shop while studying at art school and was particularly drawn to a small section of the bike industry wherein art and design were combined with a love for the bicycle.

One important aspect for Nate and Matt is that they have a cohesive and consistent work philosophy.

They believe that together they form a strong team because of their similar backgrounds, and this creative collaboration allows them to challenge and extend each other's ideas. Their artistic expertise is used to draw full-size frame drawings that are referred to during the building process to reference dimensions and clearances. "That big blank page is possibility, and the act of drawing realizes this future bicycle."

Every design decision for every bike is made with the final product in mind, and it is through exhaustive consideration of each step that Signal bikes are afforded a very deliberate, clean look. A bike will often have a final design and color scheme well before any work has begun, and it is this concept that drives Matt and Nate through to the finished product. During the building process, Nate particularly enjoys any moment when things just seem to flow naturally. He also enjoys considering the dropouts and their relationship with the stays. "The form that is created when a flat dropout is joined with a round tube is beautiful."

For Matt, one of the most exciting moments is when a bike returns from the paint shop. It feels like Christmas when the package is unwrapped to reveal their artistic designs in the fresh paintwork. Matt and Nate believe that their fine art education has given them a special understanding of form and color and how they can evoke a certain feeling or memory: "We consider the whole bicycle, not just the frame. We use our aesthetic eyes to build bicycles that make our hearts pound!"

Bike riding for both Nate and Matt is also an integral part of their business and lifestyle. Nate commutes to work and likes to get up into the mountains during summer for some single track rides. Matt races mountain bikes, does cyclocross, and a little road and track, and firmly believes that he couldn't continue building bikes if he wasn't able to experience the thrill of riding them himself.

"We consider the whole bicycle, not just the frame. We use our aesthetic eyes to build bicycles that make our hearts pound!"

"That big blank page is possibility, and the act of drawing realizes this future bicycle."

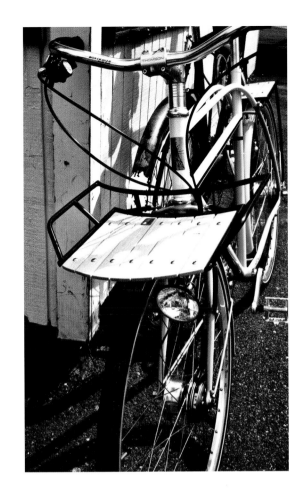

"The form that is created when a flat dropout is joined with a round tube is beautiful."

Steve Potts Bicycles

Point Reyes, California USA

Steve Potts's name is synonymous with the early development of mountain bikes and he has been building and riding bikes for 30 years. His fondest bike memory is sitting on the handlebars of his older brother's enormous paperboy bike, his brother telling him to hold on tight and get ready to break the sound barrier. When Steve reached the age of ten, he began a paper route of his own and started to explore Mount Tam, which to a ten year old was like discovering the entire world. He was the type of kid who relished the outdoors and his bike gave him the freedom to ride all over the mountain to discover creeks and waterfalls and to go fishing.

Many of Steve's skills are the product of growing up with a creative father who made a variety of objects such as telescopes, bows and arrows, musical instruments, and sailplanes. Learning from his father, and being around tools to make and repair all sorts of things, placed Steve in an environment that nurtured his natural talent for designing and building. Like many master frame builders who have built thousands of bike frames and have expertise in a range of skills, Steve Potts can build a bike from the ground up, and has done so many times.

His technical expertise is such that he is able to design and make everything from the nuts and bolts through to the bike pump, as well as designing the tires and everything in between. Although this would take hours and hours of Steve's time, he would revel in every second of it because he loves nothing more than to work with his hands and use tools and machinery to express a passionate desire to design, solve, and create.

Steve has also made the machinery and tooling equipment for the local family company that casts his head badges. Not surprisingly, the Steve Potts Bicycles head badge features Mount Tam, which was the landscape for his many adventures and a region that has vital links to the development of mountain bikes. Steve Potts was inducted into the Mountain Bike Hall of Fame in 1989 in recognition for his work as one of the early pioneers of mountain trail bikes.

As a testament to the longevity of a well-crafted handmade bike, one of Steve's fully brazed, steel cross-country mountain bikes was once checked in to his workshop to be restored. It was a bike that

he had made 25 years ago and it was fascinating for him to view his work again after all that time and to see how the bike had performed.

Steve is a sentimentalist at heart and has kept many objects that he made when he was young and proudly displays anything that his own two sons have made. He has also been known to buy back some of his bikes if given the opportunity. Steve chooses to build his mountain and road frames from titanium because of its raw beauty, mechanical properties, and non-corrosive qualities; he is also regularly called upon to restore and repair many titanium bikes from around the world. When working with titanium, the surface and environment needs to be super clean, so Steve has an ultra sonic cleaner, which he uses to clean the tubes and parts for building new bikes and restorations. The concept of a throw-away society doesn't exist in Steve Potts's world because he builds bikes that can last a lifetime, and his infectious enthusiasm for being able to make anything with his tools and machinery is only matched by his love of his family and the great outdoors.

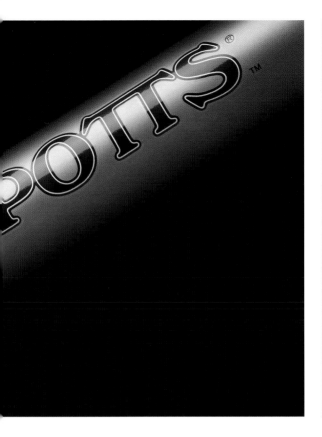

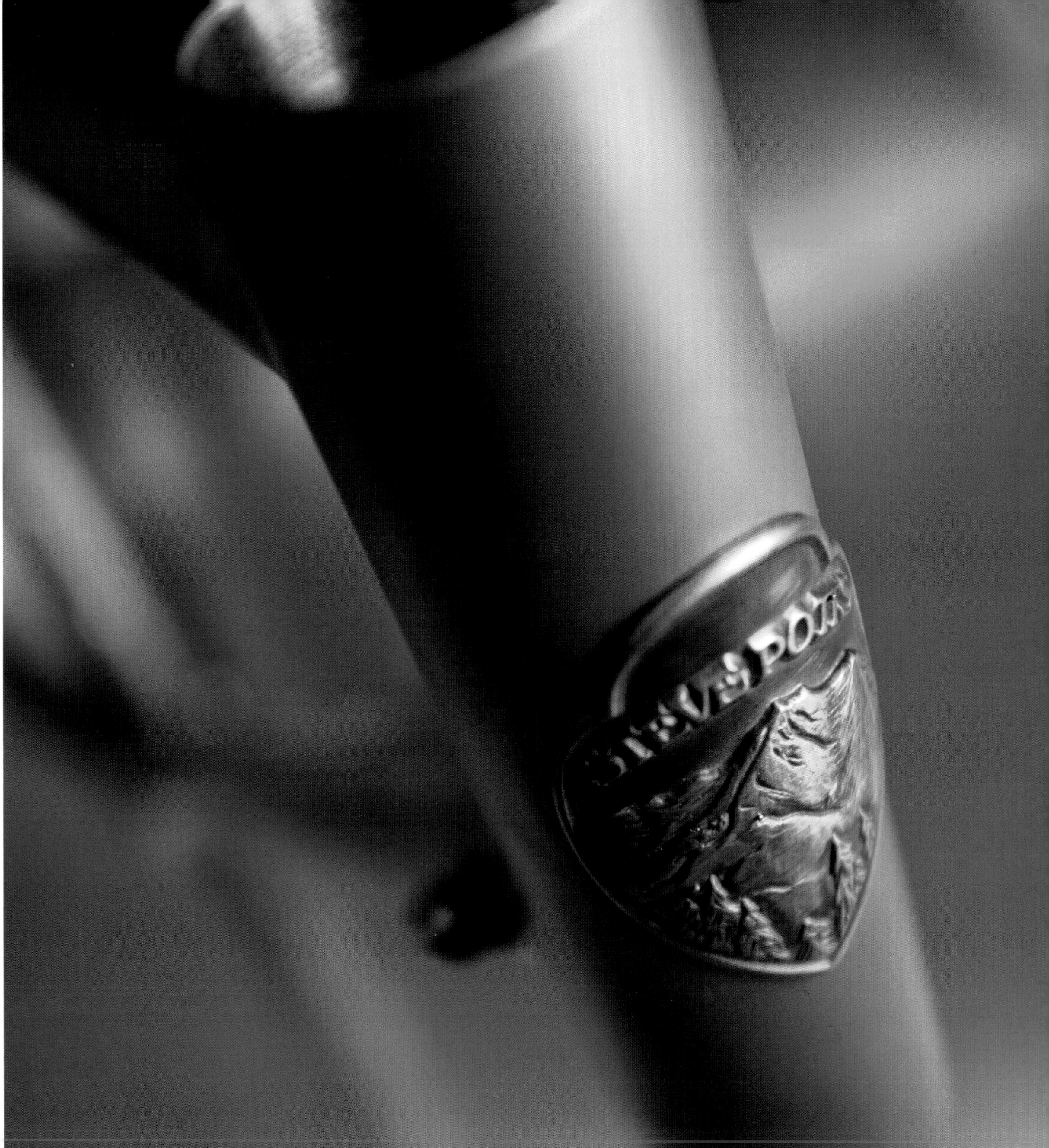

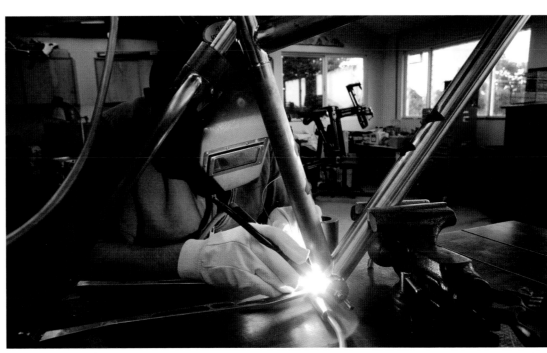

Strawberry

Portland, Oregon USA

It's a big leap from loving everything about cycling to wanting to build bike frames. For Andy Newlands, one catalyst was his love of tools. As a confirmed tool freak, the idea of collecting and using a whole range of wonderful implements to build a machine that he loved to ride was a winning combination. He'd always ridden as a kid, toured a bit, and raced, and regards cycling as the most fun you can have while staying fit.

After completing a civil engineering degree, Andy found himself in Scotland during the 1970 British Commonwealth Games and rode to Edinburgh with a bunch of cyclists. In 1971 he also rode the Tour of California in a Pacific Northwest team. It was during this tour that he spotted a bike frame that really impressed him for its workmanship and the subtle lines of the lugs and described it as being "really pretty." Andy was inspired enough to want to begin setting himself on the path to frame building and used his research time to attend bike shows in Milan and Paris to observe as many bikes as he could. Once he had sourced tools, tubing suppliers, and lugs he was ready to begin his frame-building business.

Although his father kept asking him when he was going to get a real job, Andy remained determined and just kept building steel road and track frames.

Now, 37 years on, Andy Newlands is not only a master builder but also a master toolmaker. After being in the business for so long, he's seen many advances, but considers that the bike's geometry isn't that much different. In his opinion, the most significant changes have been in steel production, which is now air hardened so it gains strength at the joint. "You braze it up around 1,500 degrees or so, and the structure is enhanced—it is actually harder and stronger at the join when it's heated to over 1,500–1,600 degrees."

When it came to choosing a name for his business Andy chose a derivative from a family name to create the name Strawberry. After visiting many bike shops in England in 1970 that were named after the owner, Andy wanted to come up with something that had a touch of humor. His grandmother was a Fraser, which comes from the French word *fraise*, meaning strawberry, so he settled on that for his company name. Andy's workspace is an old motor mechanic's garage that was built in 1948, and here he's surrounded by 2,600 square feet of tools and machinery in all shapes and sizes. While he's working, Andy likes to have music playing and confesses to knowing every Rolling Stones song ever made. As one of his friends often jokingly comments when he visits his workshop: "It's either the Rolling Stones or John Coltrane, get a life." Andy knows he has a great life—he's doing something he loves, is surrounded by a garage full of tools for his trade, and still gets out to ride for enjoyment and occasionally competes in time trials.

"You braze it up around 1,500 degrees or so, and the structure is enhanced—it's actually harder and stronger at the join when it's heated to over 1,500–1,600 degrees."

Light and tight going up ...

"A Strawberry makes it to the Col de l'Iseran, in the French Alps, September 2005. Jim Draudt, Rob Witsil, and Dave Worthington made this the highest point of many highs during a week riding through the Alps. The Strawberry was fantastic, light and tight going up and rock solid going down."

Jim Draudt, Portland Oregon

Vanilla Bicycles

Portland, Oregon USA

Located in an old milking parlor of Portland's Belmont Dairy building, the understated Vanilla signage welcomes people who have sought them out, without attracting too much attention from the general public. Customers are often first drawn to Vanilla Bicycles for their aesthetic qualities, from the color palettes to the use of raw metal to complement painted portions, right down to the overall shape of the bike being balanced and "right." After the initial connection with the aesthetics, the unique qualities of a Vanilla bike can be found below the surface, where many of the aesthetic, sexy touches also have purpose. It is this level of detail that allows the customer to form a close relationship with their Vanilla.

The creator and owner of Vanilla Bicycles, Sacha White, is driven by the challenge to do better today than he did yesterday. This philosophy extends from craftsmanship to design and business, through to taking good care of his clients. "I always try to improve on what I've done before. Each new bike or concept stands on the shoulders of what I have done in the past and what my mentors have done before me." Sacha stands by the adage that there

is potential for greatness everywhere we look and is a firm believer that it's not the material or method of construction used, but what the builder does with his given materials.

Sacha's choice of material is steel because it is what he started working with and is the medium with which he refined his bike building skills. He's the sole builder at Vanilla and is fortunate to have a handful of great people who take care of the peripheral tasks. His role at Vanilla includes being the fit specialist, designer, and frame builder, while Scott, his assistant, preps the frames for paint and polishes stainless, and also takes care of packing and shipping, customer service, parts ordering, and bike builds.

The Vanilla workspace is also a reflection of the way Sacha White likes to conduct his business: "It has always been important to me that when someone comes to visit Vanilla, they are welcomed into a beautiful space. A space that really represents Vanilla's world." Inside, the customer enters a refined, but rustic environment where they can view Vanilla bicycles in the boutique showroom.

For the measuring process there is a dedicated private fitting area and a separate design and office space to discuss ideas. The workshop section at the rear of the building is where all of the metal fabrication takes place.

In the 10 years that Sacha has been creating Vanilla bicycles he has found that the subtle nuances of construction and alignment always hold an opportunity for improvement. He enjoys dissecting his processes and putting the pieces back together to create something more ideal. One feature that he is particularly proud of is the integrated braking system of the Speedvagen Cyclocross bikes because it's a feature that he's never seen on another bike and believes that it is a real improvement on the traditional system. Sacha rides bikes as a form of transport to get both himself and his family around, and also likes to race cyclocross and ride with friends and the Vanilla team. When he's not spending time with his family, creating bikes or cycling, you can be sure that Sacha is taking time out to dream of new projects.

"It has always been important to me that when someone comes to visit Vanilla, they are welcomed into a beautiful space. A space that really represents Vanilla's world."

"I always try to improve on what I've done before. Each new bike or concept stands on the shoulders of what I have done in the past and what my mentors have done before me."

Vendetta Cycles

Willamette Valley, Oregon USA

Vendetta Cycles is very much about two guys making beautiful objects that make people smile. A combination of degrees in mechanical engineering and metallurgy along with an acetylene torch, found Conor Buescher and Garrett Clark establishing a business in 2004. Building custom bicycles allowed them to combine engineering know-how, practical experience, and dedication to the craftsmanship of lugged-steel bikes. Conor had many years experience riding, racing, and selling bikes, whereas Garrett's interests had been in all things mechanical and the hobby of motor racing. Conor and Garrett are thoroughly dedicated to building lugged bikes and believe the real spirit of the bicycle is seen in the lugs, which are the confluence of the three most important features of Vendetta bikes—function, craftsmanship, and beauty.

In terms of functionality, lugs provide structural reinforcement in the most heavily stressed part of the bike. Craftsmanship is expressed in the edges of the lugs, where brazed shorelines should be crisp and smooth, because they show the skill of the constructor. And for sheer beauty, the pointy shape of the lugs is primarily intended to smooth the structural transition from the lug to the tube, and this goal can be met with an infinite variety of artfully designed shapes. Their devotion to lugs is equaled by an enthusiasm for building with steel, which perfectly matches their design philosophy because of its high strength and excellent formability. It also allows for thin tube walls that ensure a lightweight bicycle with excellent riding characteristics. Steel is also compatible with their preferred joining technique of silver-brazing and lugged construction.

Conor and Garrett confer on every aspect of each frame design and construction. They are so committed to this approach that both must approve every part of the design, construction, and finish work. It makes for very vibrant discussions and critical analysis of every decision, but they also have their areas of expertise. "I think you can say we have a lot of fun at work, and that simultaneously respectful and irreverent attitude can be seen in the unique quality of our work." Classic rock of the 1960s and 70s such as Led Zeppelin can be heard as a backdrop to their lively debates, although they sometimes stretch themselves to the 90s with some Pacific Northwest grunge rock. The entire building process has many great moments for them both: "Once the lug carving is complete, the true soul of the bike is identifiable. Once the major tubes have been joined, the complete structure is visible. When the polishing and paint are done the feeling is not unlike a birthday." Their favorite part of the process is definitely the reaction from the bike's new owner, when they say something like: "I can tell you put a lot of love into building this bike. The ride is sublime. You've outdone yourselves." Conor and Garrett start their typical working day by going to their day jobs. They both work full-time as engineers and pursue their love of custom bike building after hours and on weekends. In between working full-time and building bikes, Conor is also a movie buff and has written and directed several films, including an award-winning comedic short. Garrett also continues to participate in his hobby of motor racing. "Keeping up with building bikes, day jobs, families and hobbies can really wear a guy out," but they wouldn't have it any other way.

"Once the lug carving is complete, the true soul of the bike is identifiable. Once the major tubes have been joined, the complete structure is visible. When the polishing and paint are done the feeling is not unlike a birthday."

The bike sings …

"The bike rides like a dream, super smooth and stable at every speed. I've taken her out on numerous club rides, you know the kind, where all the carbon and titanium frames come out to play. Everybody is blown away by the beauty and handmade craftsmanship. The fork whistles in the pitch of d# at the right speed, so I guess the bike sings."

Gary Schmid

Vicious Cycles

New Paltz, New York USA

Carl Schlemowitz believes that there's a moment in time for some people when cycling transcends sport and becomes a lifestyle. It begins to permeate all areas of their life and they tend to live and breathe everything cycling-related: these are the kind of customers who are attracted to owning a custom-made bicycle from Vicious Cycles.

For Carl, cycling is a simple and fun thing to do, but importantly it is also emotionally and spiritually fulfilling: "Some people say it's kind of like meditating when they're out for a ride." When it came to choosing a name for his company 13 years ago, Carl Schlemowitz chose Vicious Cycles because of the potential for multiple interpretations. He liked the idea that a bike has the ability to take people away from whatever vicious cycle may be pushing them down in life. Alternatively, it could also refer to the aggression needed by a rider and their bike to navigate over bumpy mountain biking terrains.

Carl feels that cycling is more than just fun—it is also a very liberating experience. He believes that riding offers people a sense of freedom and appreciates the historical link that bicycles have with the women's suffrage movement. The bicycle became a symbol of liberation for many women fighting for the right to vote, and a large number of women gained a certain sense of independence by taking up riding as a form of transport.

When building a bike for a customer, the passion that Carl and his team have for cycling extends through to the creative construction and finishing touches. From an artistic background, Carl was keen to use his creativity in the design and construction of his bikes, which are also widely appreciated for their innovative and high-quality paint designs. Vicious Cycles can turn a simple bike frame into a traveling piece of art. Carl is also dedicated to continually testing new technological developments and striving to improve Vicious Cycles' bike designs and processes.

The Vicious Cycles team produces a range of steel and titanium bikes, including road, touring, mountain, and cyclocross, which are all made by hand at the Vicious Cycles workshop. The team would not be complete without Shayla, who plays an integral part in the production of every Vicious Cycles bike. Shayla is Carl's 14-year-old Alaskan Husky, who was just a puppy when Carl established Vicious Cycles. He decided that her image would make a good head badge for his bikes, and her likeness has been included on every bicycle that Vicious Cycles has produced.

"Some people say it's kind of like meditating when they're out for a ride."

Wolfhound Cycles

Talent, Oregon USA

After graduating from college with a health promotions degree in 1998, Fred Cuthbert struggled to find a vocation that would keep him creatively satisfied and also physically active. It was a developing love for mountain biking that would eventually lead him to building bikes. Fred was drawn to the process of designing and creating custom bicycles because it enabled him to work as both craftsman and artist, combining mechanical functionality with art in design.

When Fred started building bikes in 2001, he owned a Wolfhound called Duncan. Fred not only thought that this provided the perfect name for his business, but he also decided to design the Wolfhound head badge in the dog's likeness. Sadly, Duncan has since passed away, but Fred has another Wolfhound who is carrying on the tradition. Fred's workspace is a cargo trailer with a tall roof, located in his backyard. Once he enters his "box" each morning, the music is the first thing that is turned on, which is another passion in his life.

When it comes to custom-made bikes, Fred believes that no-one should ever buy such a specialized and expensive piece of equipment as his or her first bike. Therefore, most of his customers are experienced riders who come to him already knowing exactly what they want in a bike, and in some cases have already pre-prepared all their measurements. Fred considers it important to evaluate each client's current bike and engages his customers with a thorough consultation to discover their preferred riding characteristics and style. Many customers are seriously involved in cycling and are often seeking extremely specific elements in their custom bikes.

Fred believes that most people appreciate and understand the time that goes into designing and building a custom bike because they are just as passionate about their riding as he is about his building: "To me, the process of building a bike is indeed an art, and nothing exemplifies this art more than a beautifully brazed bike." Fred considers it

a huge compliment to be able to build someone the primary machine for what is usually his or her greatest passion. Sometimes the wait list for a Wolfhound bike can be several months, but for Fred, finding people that don't mind waiting is actually an inspiring thing. His clients want a bike with individuality, to have a point of difference, and to know that the bike has been specifically fitted and made for them alone. Fred Cuthbert feels incredibly fortunate to be able to pursue his passion for bicycles, because he can't imagine doing anything else.

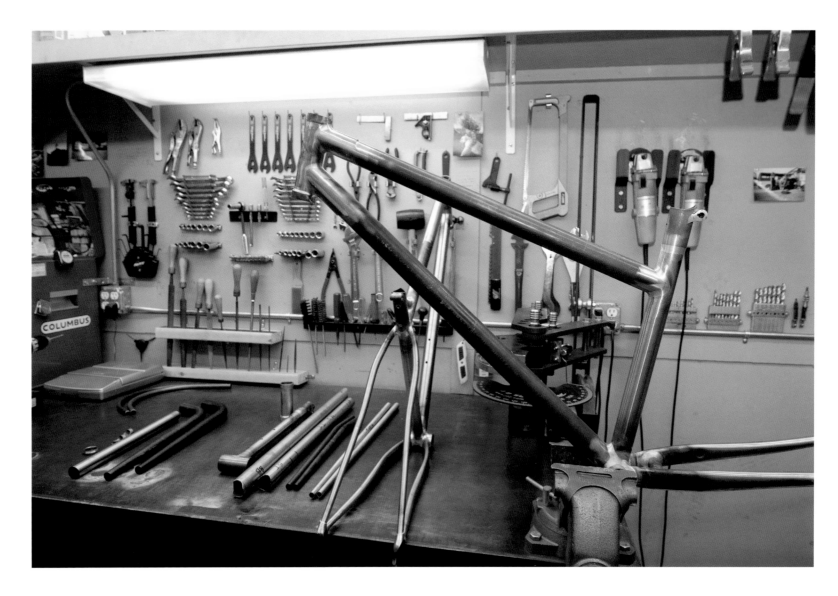

"To me, the process of building a bike is indeed an art, and nothing exemplifies this art more than a beautifully brazed bike."

It wanted to get up the hill faster than I did …

"I finally got to ride my new Wolfhound—it is a sweet ride all round. I made sure to hit my favorite downhill section and it descended beautifully—the rear end is stiff, but forgiving. The placement of the rear wheel feels just right, the bike's geometry allows my legs to soak up bumps in a very natural motion, giving a nice smooth ride through the rough stuff. In the tight and twisties, it held its line really well and shot out of the corners. On the climb, it was incredibly responsive; with every pedal stroke I could feel the tire literally pushing me up the hill, it wanted to get up the hill faster than I did. I have loved working with Fred … absolutely awesome!"

Zach Morrow

Contact details

Anderson Custom Bicycles
www.andersoncustombicycles.com

Bruce Gordon Cycles
www.bgcycles.com

Don Walker Cycles
www.donwalkercycles.com

Atum22
www.atum22.com

Calfee Design
www.calfeedesign.com

GURU Bikes
www.gurubikes.com

Baum Cycles
www.baumcycles.com

Columbine Cycle Works
www.columbinecycle.com

Independent Fabrication
www.ifbikes.com

Bilenky Cycle Works
www.bilenky.com

Crisp Titanium
www.crisptitanium.com

Ira Ryan Cycles
www.iraryancycles.com

Black Sheep Bikes
www.blacksheepbikes.com

Cycles Alex Singer
www.cycles-alex-singer.fr

Jeff Jones Custom Bicycles
www.jonesbikes.com

Bob Brown Cycles
www.bobbrowncycles.com

Cyfac
www.cyfac.fr

Keith Anderson Cycles
www.keithandersoncycles.com

Bohemian Bicycles
www.bohemianbicycles.com

Davidson Handbuilt Bicycles
www.davidsonbicycles.com

Kirk Frameworks
www.kirkframeworks.com

Kish Fabrication
www.kishbike.com

Pegoretti
www.pegoretticicli.com

Vanilla Bicycles
www.vanillabicycles.com

Llewellyn Custom Bicycles
www.llewellynbikes.com

Richard Sachs Cycles
www.richardsachs.com

Vendetta Cycles
www.vendettacycles.com

Luna Cycles
www.lunacycles.com

Roark Custom Titanium Bicycles
www.roarkcycles.com

Vicious Cycles
www.viciouscycles.com

Lynskey
www.lynskeyperformance.com

Robin Mather
www.robinmathercycles.co.uk

Wolfhound Cycles
www.wolfhoundcycles.com

Marschall Framework
www.marschall-framework.de

Signal Cycles
www.signalcycles.com

Moots
www.moots.com

Steve Potts Bicycles
www.stevepottsbicycles.com

Naked Bicycles and Design
www.timetogetnaked.com

Strawberry
www.strawberrybicycle.com

Photography credits

Introduction

Page 8: Nate Armbrust

Page 9: Craig Mole, courtesy Brett Horton

Page 10 (top left): Mike Hills

Page 10 (top right and bottom): Calfee Design

Page 11 (top): Dean Bentley

Page 11 (bottom): Jeff Jones

Anderson Custom Bicycles

All images: courtesy Anderson Custom Bicycles

Atum22

All images: courtesy Atum22; except page 21
Ges Payne

Baum Cycles

Pages 23, 24 (top left and top right), 26, 27, 28, 29:
Robert Zappulla

Pages 24 (bottom left and bottom right), 29:
courtesy Baum Cycles

Bilenky Cycle Works

Page 31: Russ Roca

Page 32 (right): Jack Ramsdale

Page 32 (left): courtesy Bilenky Cycle Works

Page 33 (top left and top right): Ken Toda

Page 33 (bottom left): Matt Ramano

Page 33 (bottom right): Allan Rodzinski

Black Sheep Bikes

All images: Dan Bailey

Bob Brown Cycles

All images: Bob Brown

Bohemian Bicycles

Pages 45, 47 (bottom): Kathi Moore

Page 46: Nick Jensen

Page 47 (top): courtesy Bohemian Bicycles

Bruce Gordon Cycles

All images: Matthew Farruggio

Calfee Design

All images: courtesy Calfee Design

Columbine Cycle Works

Pages 63, 65 (left): Brian McDivitt Photography

Pages 64, 65 (top left and bottom left): Milt Borchert

Crisp Titanium

Pages 67, 68 (bottom), 69 (top left, top right):
Gabriele Galimberti

Pages 68 (top), 70, 71: courtesy Crisp Titanium

Page 69 (bottom left and bottom right): ORME.TV

Cycles Alex Singer

Pages 73, 75 (top right and bottom):
Jean-Pierre Praderes

Page 74: courtesy Cycles Alex Singer

Cyfac

Pages 77, 81: Matthew McKee

Pages 78, 80: Eric Despin – Kalimaj

Page 79: Patrick De Coninck

Davidson Handbuilt Bicycles

All images: Bill Davidson

Don Walker Cycles

All images: Joe Vondersaar

GURU Bikes

Pages 93, 95 (bottom right), 96, 97: Studio Pettas

Pages 94, 95 (top left, top right, bottom left):
Maurice Richichi

Independent Fabrication

All images: courtesy Independent Fabrication

Ira Ryan Cycles

All photos: Nate Armbrust

Jeff Jones Custom Bicycles

Pages 111, 112 (top left), 113, 114: Tim Tidball

Pages 112 (top right and bottom left), 115, 116, 117
(left and top right): Jeff Jones

Page 112 (bottom right): Sheila Jones

Page 117 (bottom left): Jonathan Bacon

Keith Anderson Cycles

All images: Keith Anderson

Kirk Frameworks

All images: David Kirk; except page 124
(bottom right) Karin Kirk

Kish Fabrication

All images: Colin Michael Photography

Llewellyn Custom Bicycles

All images: Journey of Life Photography

Luna Cycles

All images: Margo Conover

Lynskey

All images: Jamie Pillsbury

Marschall Framework

All images: Klaus Schneider

Moots

Pages 157, 158, 159 (bottom right): Michael Robson

Pages 159 (top and bottom left), 160, 161 (bottom):
Dave Epperson

Page 161 (top): Mike Curiak

Naked Bicycles and Design

All images: Sam Whittington; except page 163
Andrea Blaseckie

Pegoretti

Pages 167, 168 (bottom), 169, 170, 171, 173:
Herman Seidl Tirez

Page 168 (top left, top center, top right):
courtesy Pegoretti

Page 172: Gita Sporting Goods Ltd

Richard Sachs Cycles

Pages 175, 176 (top), 178, 179: Jeff Weir
Photography

Pages 176 (bottom left), 177 (bottom right):
Richard Sachs

Page 176 (bottom right): MLK Images

Page 177 (top): Michael Johnson Photography

Page 177 (bottom left): Caryn Davis Photography

Roark Custom Titanium Bicycles

Pages 181, 184, 185: Brad Quartuccio

Pages 182, 183: Farid A. Abraham

Robin Mather

All images: Robin Mather

Signal Cycles

Pages 195, 196, 197, 198, 199, 200: Mike Hills

Page 201: Matt Cardinal

Steve Potts Bicycles

Pages 203, 204 (left and top right), 207 (top), 208,
209 (top right): Dean Bentley

Pages 204 (bottom right), 205 (top right): Steve Potts

Pages 205 (bottom), 206, 207 (bottom left and
bottom right), 209 (bottom right): Stuart Schwartz

Strawberry

Page 211: Joe Hawes, Flash Pro

Page 212 (bottom): David Jablonka

Pages 212 (top), 213: Andy Newlands

Vanilla Bicycles

Pages 215, 218, 219: Craig Mole,
courtesy Brett Horton

Pages 216, 217: Robert M. Huff

Vendetta Cycles

Pages 221, 223 (left): Tina Buescher Photography

Pages 222, 223 (right and bottom right):
courtesy Vendetta Cycles

Vicious Cycles

Page 225: Sean Davis

Page 226 (top left and top right): Sean Davis

Page 226 (bottom): Marco Quezada

Page 227: courtesy Vicious Cycles

Wolfhound Cycles

All images: Sean Bagshaw; except page 230
Jason Van Horn Photography